Revolutions In Steel

Revolutions In Steel

India's Industrial Journey

Sam Loray

UNIEK ENTERPRISES

CONTENTS

INDEX

Chapter 7: "Global Partnerships and Trade"

7.1 The international dynamics of India's steel trade.

7.2 The significance of global market integration.

7.3 Challenges and opportunities in a competitive global market.

Introduction

The narrative of India's modern process is one of noteworthy change and commotion. From a land well established in conventional agrarian economies, India has seen a progression of upheavals that have slung it into the worldwide spotlight as a thriving modern force to be reckoned with. At the core of this change lies the steel business, an area that has been a key part in India's modern development, molding its financial, social, and political scenes. This story expects to dig into the multi-layered parts of India's steel industry, following its beginnings, investigating its critical minutes, and examining its commitments to the nation's development and advancement.

By and large, India's relationship with steel goes back centuries. The foundations of iron and steel creation can be followed to the old city of Mohenjo-Daro, where early developments showed a momentous capability in metallurgy. In any case, it was only after the English frontier time that the Indian steel industry saw huge modernization and development. The foundation of Goodbye Iron and Steel Organization (TISCO) in 1907 by Jamsetji Goodbye denoted a critical defining moment. TISCO's outcome in creating great steel assumed a crucial part in catalyzing India's modern transformation, an establishment whereupon the country's ensuing modern excursion would be fabricated.

The many years following India's freedom in 1947 were set apart by a conscious spotlight on confidence and weighty industrialization. Under the initiative of Jawaharlal Nehru, India looked to construct a communist situated economy, with the steel business at its center. The foundation of the Bhilai, Rourkela, and Durgapur steel plants during the 1950s laid the basis for huge scope homegrown steel creation. These drives, known as the 'Hindu Pace of Development,' set before India the way to independence and steel industry extension. The gigantic Bhilai Steel Plant, for example, arose as a symbol of this period, altogether adding to the country's foundation improvement.

The 1991 monetary changes, initiated by then-Money Priest Dr. Manmohan Singh, proclaimed another period in India's modern scene. These changes destroyed the 'Permit Raj' and opened the entryways for unfamiliar speculation and progression. The steel business, in the same way as other different areas, was significantly affected.

The public authority diminished its control and permitted private players to enter the market, prodding rivalry and advancement. This change rejuvenated the current steel monsters as well as prepared for new participants, prompting a more powerful and internationally cutthroat industry.

Quite possibly of the main achievement in the steel business' cutting edge history was the ascent of the Mittal family, with Lakshmi Mittal at its rudder. Lakshmi Mittal's ArcelorMittal turned into a worldwide steel monster, a demonstration of Indian business and the developing global impact of the Indian diaspora. Mittal's story isn't only one of business insight yet additionally an image of the Indian steel industry's possible on the worldwide stage.

India's steel industry, driven by both public and confidential undertakings, went through significant changes in the 21st 100 years. The extension of existing plants and the foundation of new ones mirrored India's flooding interest for steel, driven by framework advancement, urbanization, and the development of the vehicle area. Steel became key for building the advanced India, from high rises in metropolitan communities to the development of roadways and extensions associating far off towns.

However, close by this development, difficulties and intricacies emerged. Ecological worries, land procurement debates, and issues connected with work privileges arose as huge obstacles to feasible development. The business needed to explore a fragile harmony between satisfying developing need and the need to address the natural and social results of its activities basic. Government strategies and guidelines assumed a significant part in molding this scene, with drives like the Public Steel Strategy underscoring feasible practices and dependable modern development.

Moreover, India's steel industry has not been insusceptible to the back and forth movements of the worldwide market. Cost vacillations, exchange questions, and monetary slumps have all affected the area, impacting venture choices and business techniques. The flexibility and versatility of the business have been tried consistently, as it endeavors to stay serious and pertinent in the always changing worldwide steel market.

The computerized age brought new open doors and difficulties for the steel business. Innovation driven advancements, for example, Industry 4.0 and robotization, upset assembling processes, prompting expanded proficiency and accuracy. These headways can possibly additionally drive India's steel industry into the future by upgrading efficiency and decreasing natural impressions. The progress to green and economical steel creation has additionally picked up speed, lining up with worldwide endeavors to battle environmental change. India's steel industry isn't simply a monetary power yet a central member in tending to natural and manageability concerns.

In the midst of this large number of changes, recognizing the human element of the steel industry is basic. The labor force, from the excavators to the architects, plays had an instrumental impact in molding the business' direction. Trade guilds, their battles, and their commitments have been basic to the steel business' story, mirroring the more extensive work development in India. The development of work practices, privileges, and conditions throughout the long term reflects the social and monetary movements inside the area.

The steel business isn't simply a story of financial development and improvement; it is interwoven with India's political scene. It has been a wellspring of government income, business, and modern advancement. Political choices, strategy changes, and economic deals have all impacted the direction of the steel area. Understanding this relationship is vital in fathoming the business' job in forming India's political economy.

India's steel industry has not recently been a financial huge advantage; it has likewise been a social image and a wellspring of pride for the country. The notorious Passage of India in Mumbai, the gigantic Sardar Vallabhbhai Patel Sculpture of Solidarity in Gujarat, and endless other compositional wonders have been made conceivable by the business' commitments. Steel's flexibility and strength have fabricated framework as well as become significant of India's own excursion from pioneer enslavement to post-freedom progress.

The interconnectedness of the steel business with India's modern, monetary, social, and political aspects couldn't possibly be more significant. As the nation proceeds with its way of monetary development and worldwide reconciliation, the steel business stays a significant component of India's character and desires. Nonetheless, it faces a future loaded up with the two valuable open doors and difficulties. Adjusting the requirement for expanded creation with maintainability, guaranteeing the prosperity of the labor force, and adjusting to the consistently developing worldwide market are only a couple of the intricate issues that the business should explore.

With regards to the computerized age and ecological cognizance, the steel business is near the very edge of another upheaval. Developments in materials, creation strategies, and the rise of round economies are reshaping the scene. The change from conventional steel to cutting edge materials and advancements will be a basic piece of India's modern process in the next few decades. The incorporation of man-made reasoning, computerization, and maintainable practices will characterize the business' future, permitting it to address the difficulties of the 21st 100 years.

The worldwide energy progress and the requirement for decarbonization likewise present an existential test and a chance for the steel business. Adjusting to cleaner and more feasible techniques for creation is fundamental to alleviate the ecological effect of steelmaking. India's steel industry, in arrangement with its responsibilities under global environment arrangements, should graph a way towards greener practices, from natural substance extraction to the end result. This progress isn't simply a financial basic however a moral and ecological commitment.

To comprehend the full extent of India's modern process through its steel industry, one should investigate the encounters of the various partners included. It incorporates the industry moguls and policymakers as well as the specialists, the networks, the natural activists, and the purchasers. Their voices and encounters are indispensable to the account, as they shape the business' direction and its effect on society at large.

Unrests In Steel: India's Modern Process is a profound investigation of a powerful area that has gone through numerous transformations, continually adjusting to new difficulties and open doors. An excursion navigates reality, from the old foundations of metallurgy to the state of the art innovations of the current day. The account looks to catch the pith of the steel business' past, present, and future, revealing its multi-faceted effect on the nation and the world.

In the pages that follow, we will dig into the authentic groundworks of India's steel industry and follow its development through critical minutes and groundbreaking periods. We will investigate the monetary and political powers that have impacted the business' direction and its social and ecological repercussions. We will analyze the job of innovation and development in forming the business' present and future. We will likewise examine the difficulties and potential open doors confronting the area in the 21st hundred years.

Chapter 1

"The Genesis of Industry"

The beginning of industry is a mind boggling story that follows mankind's movement from crude economies to the complex, mechanically determined frameworks of the cutting edge period. A story unfurls across hundreds of years, formed by a mixture of cultural, monetary, mechanical, and social factors that have catalyzed the development of industry.

The beginning of industry can be followed back to the actual underpinnings of human advancement. In the antiquated world, early human social orders depended on agrarian practices for food, developing the land and receiving its benefits. As these social orders developed and create, the requirement for specific exchanges arose, bringing about simple types of industry. Craftspeople and craftsmans created instruments, ceramics, and materials, denoting the underlying strides towards specific creation.

The beginning of the Modern Unrest in the late eighteenth century lighted a significant and irreversible change. The development of motorized processes, similar to the steam motor, denoted a seismic change in assembling and creation. This period proclaimed the shift from agrarian and handmade economies to automated, manufacturing plant based creation, fundamentally expanding proficiency and result.

Mechanical advancements kept on molding the direction of industry. Headways in steel creation, the tackling of power, and the improvement of mechanical production system methods by visionaries like Henry Passage further upset assembling. Large scale manufacturing turned into the standard, working with the making of merchandise on an uncommon scale.

At the same time, urbanization and the foundation of enormous scope processing plants drew millions from country regions to urban areas, making way for cultural and segment shifts. It changed how products were created as well as modified the scene of human existence and work. Industrial facilities became centers of business, moving monetary development yet additionally presenting new difficulties like work double-dealing and unfortunate working circumstances.

The development of industry isn't just restricted to assembling. The coming of the Data Age moved another flood of change. The ascent of PCs and the web has reshaped business, correspondence, and creation techniques. Ideas like robotization, man-made reasoning, and mechanical technology have modified the modern scene, expanding proficiency and accuracy while suggesting conversation starters about the eventual fate of human work.

Globalization, couple with mechanical advancement, has associated markets around the world, empowering the consistent progression of products, administrations, and thoughts across borders. This interconnectedness has extended markets as well as introduced difficulties, like financial reliance, international intricacies, and natural worries emerging from expanded creation and utilization.

The beginning of industry hasn't been without its repercussions. The ecological effect of industrialization is a squeezing concern. The extraction of normal assets, contamination, and the discharge of ozone depleting substances have added to environmental change and natural corruption, requiring pressing intercessions and a shift towards manageable practices.

The development of industry has likewise prompted critical changes in cultural designs and values. The ascent of commercialization, driven by the accessibility of efficiently manufactured products, has affected ways of life and utilization designs, frequently prompting banters about realism and its effect on individual prosperity and cultural qualities.

The connection among industry and society isn't one-layered. It's an intricate transaction of financial matters, innovation, culture, and governmental issues. Advancements in industry have set off friendly unrests, changed power elements, and reclassified monetary frameworks. From mercantilism to private enterprise, the idea of economies and the dispersion of abundance has consistently developed, forming the texture of social orders.

Moreover, industry has been an impetus for progressions in medical care, schooling, and by and large ways of life. The excess created from industrialization has supported logical exploration, foundation improvement, and social government assistance programs, adding to upgraded personal satisfaction for some.

In addition, the effect of industry stretches out past the unmistakable domain. It has affected craftsmanship, writing, and mainstream society. The symbolism of manufacturing plants and apparatus has been deified in imaginative articulations, reflecting both the wonderment and nervousness that this extraordinary power has evoked in human personalities.

The direction of industry is a powerful continuum, formed by development, guideline, and cultural reactions. State run administrations and worldwide bodies have interceded through strategies and guidelines to deal with the effect of modern exercises, underscoring maintainability, laborer freedoms, and natural preservation.

Looking forward, the eventual fate of industry holds both commitment and difficulties. Ideas like Industry 4.0, portrayed via robotization, large information, and the Web of Things, predict another period of modern development. The combination of these advancements might smooth out processes, increment efficiency, and usher in additional opportunities, yet it likewise brings up issues about the fate of work and the potential for additional cultural variations.

The beginning of industry is a legendary story, denoting the rising of humankind from means to excess, from craftsmanship to large scale manufacturing, and from segregated economies to an internationally interconnected world. Its effect on progress is significant and diverse, molding economies as well as social orders, societies, and the actual texture of human life.

1.1 Introduction to the significance of industrialization in India.

Industrialization plays had a crucial impact in molding the fate of countries across the globe. With regards to India, a country famous for its rich history, different culture, and old civilization, the excursion of industrialization conveys colossal importance. It addresses monetary advancement as well as friendly, political, and social change. The narrative of industrialization in India is a diverse story, set apart by wins, challenges, and a steadfast soul of flexibility.

India's industrialization process can't be grasped in disconnection from its authentic foundation. The subcontinent has a long and recognized history of business and craftsmanship, with proof of cutting edge metallurgy, materials, and different enterprises going back millennia. The Indus Valley Human progress, for example, was a center of refined metropolitan preparation and modern exercises.

Notwithstanding, the beginning of English frontier rule in the eighteenth century significantly affected India's financial scene. The pilgrim period saw a critical change in India's monetary needs, with the English Realm taking advantage of the nation's assets and diverting them to fulfill its own modern needs. This period acquainted India with present day industry, yet the advantages gathered lopsidedly to the provincial power. Indian culture was changed, yet the change was damaged by double-dealing, destitution, and reliance.

It was against this scenery that India's battle for autonomy started, with pioneers like Mahatma Gandhi underscoring monetary independence and the significance of reviving native enterprises. The year 1947 denoted a defining moment in India's set of experiences as the nation acquired its hard-battled freedom from English rule. This pivotal event was joined by the beginning of another time of country building and a dream for financial independence.

Post-autonomy, the Indian government perceived the essential job of industrialization in cultivating monetary development and cultural turn of events. A progression of Five-Year Plans were started, zeroing in on key areas like weighty industry, framework, and farming, making way for India's industrialization. The making of public area endeavors and the accentuation on import replacement were a portion of the key systems utilized during this period.

One of the famous images of India's industrialization drive during the mid-twentieth century was the foundation of the Bhilai Steel Plant in 1955, a demonstration of the country's assurance to foster its weighty industry. This obvious the start of a progression of huge modern tasks, including the development of dams, roadways, and the extension of the public area.

Nonetheless, the way to industrialization was not without its difficulties. India confronted imperatives like restricted monetary assets, obsolete framework, and the need to construct human resources. Conquering these obstacles required a blend of key preparation, speculations, and strategy measures.

The 1991 monetary progression denoted a turning point in India's industrialization process. The public authority started a progression of changes pointed toward opening up the economy, decreasing state control, and advancing confidential area cooperation. This change made ready for expanded unfamiliar venture and incorporation into the worldwide economy, prompting higher development rates and mechanical headways.

India's progress in the IT and programming administrations industry turned into a worldwide peculiarity, moving the country into the class of arising monetary powers. This advancement exemplified the extraordinary capability of industrialization and innovation in the cutting edge period.

Moreover, India's industrialization process is set apart by provincial varieties and inconsistencies. While states like Maharashtra, Tamil Nadu, and Karnataka have been at the front of industrialization, districts like the northeastern states and a few pieces of northern India face huge difficulties in finding the industrialization wave. These incongruities highlight the requirement for evenhanded and comprehensive modern turn of events.

The meaning of industrialization in India goes past financial development. It has significant ramifications for the social texture of the country. Industrialization has been an impetus for urbanization, with millions relocating from country regions to urban communities looking for work open doors. This segment shift has achieved changes in ways of life, everyday environments, and social elements.

Simultaneously, industrialization has added to enhancements in schooling and medical care, as the excess produced from financial exercises has subsidized social government assistance projects and foundation advancement. The development of enterprises has encouraged an interest for talented work, prompting an extension of instructive organizations and professional instructional hubs.

The job of ladies in the Indian labor force has additionally advanced with industrialization. Ladies have progressively turned into a piece of the proper workforce, breaking conventional generalizations and adding to family livelihoods. The changing job of ladies in the labor force has upgraded financial success as well as encouraged orientation correspondence.

Political elements have been unpredictably connected to India's industrialization process. The country's political scene has seen changes, with industrialization impacting discretionary governmental issues and strategy needs. The requests of modern laborers and financial matters have molded political plans, prompting a harmonious connection among industrialization and administration.

Challenges, as well, have went with India's industrialization. Natural worries, work privileges, and evenhanded dissemination of abundance have been disputed matters and discussion. The journey for maintainability notwithstanding fast modern development has turned into a fundamental issue, with questions raised about the drawn out effect of industrialization on the climate and the requirement for mindful, eco-accommodating practices.

Work privileges and working circumstances have likewise involved concern. While industrialization has set out work open doors, guaranteeing fair wages and safe working circumstances has been a continuous test. The battle for laborers' freedoms, aggregate dealing, and the disposal of kid work are basic parts of India's industrialization story.

The meaning of industrialization in India stretches out to its international strategy and worldwide relations. As a rising financial power, India has effectively drawn in with the worldwide local area, fashioning vital organizations, and partaking in global economic deals. The country's modern development has situated it as a central member in the worldwide economy, drawing in unfamiliar venture and adding to discretionary talks.

The coming of the 21st century has carried new aspects to India's industrialization. Ideas like Industry 4.0, described via robotization, the Web of Things, and man-made reasoning, can possibly reshape the modern scene. India is at an intersection, confronting the test of taking on these state of the art innovations while tending to the computerized partition and guaranteeing that the advantages of such headways are comprehensive and fair.

The Coronavirus pandemic, while introducing extraordinary difficulties, additionally displayed India's modern strength. The nation adjusted to the emergency by inclining up creation of clinical supplies, antibodies, and fundamental products. The pandemic underlined the significance of a hearty medical services industry and the requirement for readiness despite worldwide difficulties.

The meaning of industrialization in India envelops a wide cluster of areas, from customary businesses like farming, materials, and assembling to present day areas like data innovation, biotechnology, and sustainable power.

The country's modern variety mirrors its yearning to accomplish independence, address the issues of its blossoming populace, and address worldwide difficulties, for example, environmental change.

Agribusiness, which has been the foundation of India's economy, is likewise complicatedly connected to industrialization. The presentation of current cultivating methods, motorization, and the improvement of agro-ventures has changed the farming scene. The Green Upheaval during the 1960s, set apart by the reception of high-yielding harvest assortments and expanded water system, fundamentally expanded food creation and assumed a pivotal part in guaranteeing food security.

The meaning of industrialization in India reaches out to the domain of framework improvement. Building powerful transportation organizations, energy networks, and correspondence frameworks has been urgent in supporting modern development. The extension of railroads, development of roadways, and modernization of ports and air terminals have worked with the development of merchandise and individuals, decreasing calculated imperatives and advancing exchange.

The energy area is one more basic feature of industrialization. The developing interest for energy has prompted interests in assorted sources, including petroleum derivatives, sustainable power, and atomic power. The quest for practical energy arrangements has acquired conspicuousness, lining up with worldwide endeavors to diminish fossil fuel byproducts and battle environmental change.

India's drug industry, frequently alluded to as the "drug store of the world," is one more demonstration of the meaning of industrialization. The nation has turned into a worldwide center for the development of reasonable prescriptions and immunizations. This industry's development has supported India's economy as well as assumed a crucial part in worldwide medical services access.

Industrialization has likewise been an impetus for examination and development. The foundation of innovative work habitats, instructive establishments, and innovation parks has sustained a culture of development. India's logical and innovative progressions .

1.2 Historical context and early industrial endeavors.

To comprehend the early modern undertakings and their verifiable setting, one should set out on an excursion through time and investigate the change of human social orders from agrarian economies to the introduction of current industry. This development was a continuous interaction set apart by key achievements and changes that had significant ramifications for mankind's monetary, social, and social scenes.

The progress from agrarian to modern social orders was a multilayered peculiarity that unfurled over hundreds of years. It was molded by a juncture of variables, including mechanical development, changes in friendly association, and the development of exchange and business. The early seeds of industrialization can be followed back to antiquated civilizations, where the underpinnings of assembling and business were laid.

One of the earliest civilizations known for its modern accomplishments was the Indus Valley Development, which flourished around 2500-1500 BCE in the Indian subcontinent. Archeological proof recommends that this old society was taken part in different types of modern exercises, for example, earthenware making, metallurgy, and material creation. The presence of cutting edge metropolitan preparation and exchange networks shows a level of monetary complexity.

Essentially, old Egypt was famous for its initial modern achievements. The development of the pyramids, a wonder of designing, involved quarrying, transportation, and development methods that expected coordinated workforces and strategic tasks. These fantastic designs served as burial places as well as images of early modern undertakings.

The Roman Realm, which traversed from the first century BCE to the fifth century CE, was one more age in the advancement of early industry. Roman designing and development procedures, including the broad street organization and reservoir conduits, exhibited the productivity and size of their modern abilities. Furthermore, the Romans presented progressions in mining, metallurgy, and the creation of cement, which lastingly affected development and framework.

The Medieval times saw the ascent of organizations, which were relationship of gifted experts and craftsmans. These societies assumed a pivotal part in the improvement of early modern exercises. They were liable for controlling creation, preparing disciples, and guaranteeing the nature of products. Organizations laid the preparation for specialization and division of work, two fundamental parts of industrialization.

In the fourteenth 100 years, the Dark Passing, an overwhelming pandemic, significantly affected European social orders. While it prompted a critical death toll, it likewise prodded changes in labor elements. The diminished populace implied that work was scant, which, thusly, expanded the worth of work. This energized mechanical advancement and automation in different businesses, like farming and materials, as individuals looked for ways of making up for the work deficiency.

The late Medieval times saw the rise of early modern exercises like material creation in Europe. The putting-out framework, otherwise called the bungalow business, was a striking turn of events. It included the dissemination of natural substances to laborers in their homes, where they would process and make merchandise. This framework established the groundwork for decentralized, limited scope modern creation, where people or families worked from their own homes.

The Renaissance time frame in the fourteenth to seventeenth hundreds of years denoted a huge change in monetary and scholarly idea. The Renaissance advanced a feeling of request and development, which added to the improvement of hardware and assembling procedures. This period additionally saw the investigation and development of shipping lanes, prompting the trading of products and thoughts between various areas of the planet.

The eighteenth century saw the start of the Modern Upset, a critical crossroads throughout the entire existence of industrialization. It was described by a progression of groundbreaking mechanical developments that pushed economies from agrarian to modern. One of the main developments of this period was the steam motor, credited to James Watt. The steam motor reformed transportation and assembling, making it conceivable to proficiently drive apparatus and trains.

The material business was quite possibly the earliest area to encounter industrialization during the late eighteenth 100 years. Developments like the turning jenny, water edge, and power loom motorized the creation of materials, prompting expanded productivity and result. The manufacturing plant framework arose as the predominant method of creation, combining laborers and machines in a concentrated area.

In equal, the iron and coal enterprises additionally went through huge changes. The purifying of iron metal with coke (a sort of coal) in impact heaters prompted an enormous expansion in iron creation. This established the groundwork for the development of the iron and steel industry, which turned into a foundation of industrialization.

The automation of horticulture was one more basic part of early industrialization. Developments like the seed drill and the mechanical gatherer worked on rural effectiveness, diminishing the work expected for cultivating. This opened up work for other modern pursuits and added to the development of metropolitan focuses.

The transportation business saw an upset with the improvement of the steam train. The main full-scale working railroad train, George Stephenson's "Motion No. 1," started activity in 1825, denoting the introduction of the rail line period. Rail lines extraordinarily upgraded the versatility of individuals and merchandise, associating far off areas and working with exchange and modern development.

The early modern undertakings additionally affected the development business. The utilization of iron and steel in the development of extensions and structures considered taller and more monstrous designs. This design development made ready for the development of high rises and huge range spans in the advanced period.

The spread of industrialization was not restricted to the Assembled Realm, where the Modern Insurgency began, yet stretched out to different pieces of Europe, North America, and ultimately, the world. Every area took on industrialization in its special manner, molded by its verifiable setting, accessible assets, and cultural variables.

In the US, the nineteenth century saw fast industrialization, driven by elements like a tremendous region, bountiful normal assets, and a developing populace. The extension of the railroad network assumed a critical part in interfacing various locales and supporting modern development. Advancements in farming, assembling, and transportation further moved the country's industrialization.

The industrialization of the US was joined by urbanization, as individuals relocated from rustic regions to urban communities looking for work potential open doors. The development of modern urban areas, like Pittsburgh, Detroit, and Chicago, became symbolic of this extraordinary period.

Also, in mainland Europe, nations like Germany and France embraced industrialization and made critical commitments to mechanical headways. The improvement of the substance business, particularly the assembling of engineered colors, and the development of the auto business were eminent accomplishments during this period.

Japan, as well, went through a momentous course of industrialization in the late nineteenth and mid twentieth hundreds of years. The Meiji Rebuilding, a political and social change, laid the foundation for Japan's modernization and industrialization. The Japanese government effectively advanced the reception of Western innovation and modern works on, prompting the fast development of ventures like materials, shipbuilding, and steel creation.

The effect of industrialization on society during this period was significant. Urbanization achieved a change in day to day environments and social designs. Assembly line laborers lived in swarmed, frequently unsanitary, metropolitan regions, confronting difficulties connected with lodging, disinfection, and admittance to fundamental conveniences. This prompted social developments upholding for work privileges and better working circumstances.

The early modern period was additionally set apart by youngster work and unfortunate working circumstances in production lines. The abuse of work, particularly ladies and youngsters, incited social change developments and the sanctioning of work regulations. The battle for laborers' privileges and the interest for more secure and more others conscious working circumstances were fundamental parts of the early industrialization stage.

While industrialization sped up monetary development, it additionally brought about imbalances. The proprietors of processing plants and businesses, frequently alluded to as the industrialist class, aggregated significant riches and influence. This abundance uniqueness prompted the rise of a common that confronted monetary difficulties and social minimization.

The early modern time frame was a period of huge social and political changes. The ascent of trade guilds, communist developments, and the improvement of political belief systems, for example, communism were reactions to the financial and social changes achieved by industrialization. Laborers and intelligent people started supporting for laborers' freedoms, better wages, and an impartial appropriation of abundance.

The connection among industrialization and government was additionally many-sided. The industrialized countries of Europe looked for natural substances, new business sectors, and financial open doors in different areas of the planet. This prompted pilgrim development and the enslavement of settlements to serve the financial interests of the industrialized powers.

The early modern undertakings were joined by ecological outcomes. The fast extraction of normal assets, the expansion in contamination, and the change of scenes unfavorably affected the climate. These worries foreshadowed later conversations on manageability and the requirement

1.3 The role of colonial rule in shaping India's industrial landscape.

The effect of pioneer rule on India's modern scene is an intricate and multi-layered story that traverses a few centuries. India, with its rich history, culture, and financial practices, went through huge changes during its time of pilgrim enslavement by the English Domain. This pioneer experience significantly affected India's modern turn of events, adding to the two difficulties and open doors in forming the country's modern scene.

The English provincial presence in India can be followed back to the seventeenth century when the English East India Organization laid out general stores and fortifications along the Indian shore. Over the long run, the organization extended its control, getting domains and stating authority over enormous parts of the subcontinent. The time of pioneer rule can be comprehensively partitioned into two stages: the pre-1857 period, set apart by the strength of the English East India Organization, and the post-1857 period, when India went under direct English Crown rule.

The English East India Organization, at first settled as an exchanging element, assumed a critical part in forming India's initial modern scene. The organization's activities centered around the commodity of Indian merchandise like materials, flavors, and tea to European business sectors. In doing as such, the organization laid out general stores, manufacturing plants, and strengthened settlements, in this way presenting parts of modern association in India, though on a restricted scale.

One of the prominent advancements during the pre-1857 period was the foundation of material processing plants, particularly in areas like Bengal. These plants were gotten up positioned produce materials for send out and were fueled by water wheels. The interest for Indian materials, especially cotton, was huge in European business sectors, and the English East India Organization assumed a pivotal part in working with this exchange.

In any case, the organization's presence in India was not restricted to exchange alone. It additionally controlled tremendous areas of land and removed income from the Indian populace. The arrangement of land income assortment, frequently described by shady practices, extensively affected India's agrarian economy. Subsequently, farming practices, landownership designs, and the monetary states of Indian laborers were impacted by pilgrim strategies.

The post-1857 period denoted a critical change in India's relationship with the English Domain. The Indian Defiance of 1857, frequently alluded to as the Principal Battle of Autonomy, brought about the disintegration of the English East India Organization and the exchange of power over India to the English Crown. This progress, while not essentially adjusting the idea of pilgrim rule, brought India under more straightforward control by the English government.

The pioneer rule in India was driven by monetary double-dealing. The English Domain considered India to be a wellspring of riches, and its monetary strategies were intended for extricating assets and income from the subcontinent. Land income assortment, frequently alluded to as the Long-lasting Settlement or Ryotwari Framework, was an essential component for removing abundance from India. Under these frameworks, land was surveyed, and the income was fixed, with the weight put on Indian landowners and laborers. The decent income forced an unfaltering monetary weight, frequently prompting landowners losing their properties, while workers battled to get by.

Also, the English presented cash crops like indigo, opium, and jute, which were developed for send out. The development of these money crops frequently uprooted food crops, prompting intermittent starvations and food deficiencies. The emphasis on cash crop development and the adaptation of the Indian economy changed customary agrarian practices and disturbed the harmony among agribusiness and industry.

The English provincial organization likewise assumed a part in destroying India's customary modern areas, especially in materials. The popular instance of Manchester materials represents this point. Manchester materials, delivered in Britain, were imported to India at lower costs, causing a decrease popular for Indian materials. Defensive levies and arrangements inclined toward English merchandise, antagonistically affecting the seriousness of Indian material ventures.

The presentation of English made hardware and innovation further changed India's modern scene. While it is actually the case that a few present day innovations were brought to India during pioneer rule, their basic role was to serve the interests of English industry. India was used as a wellspring of unrefined components, like cotton, and as a business opportunity for English produced merchandise, as opposed to as a center for native modern development.

The appearance of the rail route framework, albeit huge in further developing transportation and correspondence inside India, was fundamentally determined by the need to ship unrefined components productively from the hinterlands to the ports for send out. The railroads turned into an instrument of monetary double-dealing, as opposed to an impetus for India's free modern turn of events.

One more remarkable part of pioneer rule was the development of a double monetary design in India. On one hand, there was a conventional, agrarian economy that kept on giving livelihoods to most of the populace.

Then again, there was a cutting edge modern economy, which essentially served English interests and was moved in a couple of metropolitan focuses. This double monetary design made differences in riches and advancement.

The provincial period likewise had suggestions for work and modern relations in India. The frontier organization acquainted work regulations and guidelines with deal with the labor force, however these were frequently sanctioned to keep up with control and concentrate work from the populace. Numerous Indian workers, particularly in businesses like mining and estates, worked in testing conditions, frequently under abusive frameworks of agreement or fortified work.

Moreover, the pilgrim organization acquainted instructive changes that pointed with make a labor force reasonable for serving English monetary interests. While schooling was advanced, it was frequently coordinated toward creating agents and low-level representatives for the frontier organization or English claimed enterprises. This approach restricted the improvement of a talented workforce fit for driving India's free industrialization.

The effect of pilgrim rule reached out to the monetary area also. The English presented a money framework that supplanted customary types of cash and money in India. The Indian rupee turned into the standard money, and the control of cash issuance was incorporated. This gave the English specialists impressive command over India's money related strategy and monetary frameworks, which were utilized to serve pilgrim financial goals.

The monetary area likewise saw the foundation of English possessed banks and monetary organizations, which further united English financial interests in India. These foundations assumed a crucial part in working with the exchange of capital and assets from India to England.

While it is fundamental to recognize the antagonistic effect of frontier rule on India's modern scene, it is additionally critical to perceive that a few parts of modernization were presented during this period. The English presented an overall set of laws, current framework, and a simple organization, all of which assumed a part in the ensuing improvement of India. The English language likewise turned into a vehicle of guidance and organization, in the end turning into a resource for correspondence and admittance to worldwide information.

Chapter 2

"The Post-Independence Vision"

The fulfillment of freedom by India in 1947 denoted the finish of a long and turbulent frontier period and opened another part in the country's set of experiences. The post-freedom time frame gave India an exceptional chance to diagram its own course, liberated from pioneer rule, and set before out a way of country building, improvement, and self-assurance. This vision for post-freedom India incorporated a multi-layered change that crossed legislative issues, financial matters, civil rights, and industrialization.

At the center of the post-freedom vision was the foundation of a majority rule republic. India took on a majority rule arrangement of administration that underlined the standards of fairness, equity, and portrayal. The Constituent Get together of India, under the authority of Dr. B.R. Ambedkar and other noticeable pioneers, assumed a vital part in creating the Indian Constitution, which stays the directing record for the country.

The Indian Constitution cherished major privileges and opportunities for all residents, no matter what their position, statement of faith, religion, or orientation. It likewise presented an arrangement of balanced governance, a bureaucratic design of government, and a free legal executive to protect the privileges and interests of individuals. The reception of widespread grown-up testimonial considered a genuinely comprehensive and participatory majority rules system.

Financial confidence and the disposal of destitution were key parts of the post-autonomy vision. India's chiefs perceived the need to address the financial differences that had persevered during frontier rule. The Initial Five-Year Plan, started in 1951, set up for arranged monetary turn of events, accentuating farming, industry, and framework.

The vision of confidence was caught in State head Jawaharlal Nehru's call for "logical attitude" and the improvement of native enterprises. The foundation of public area undertakings, for example, the Steel Authority of India Restricted (SAIL), the Oil and Flammable gas Organization (ONGC), and the Public Nuclear energy Enterprise (NTPC), mirrored the obligation to decreasing reliance on imported products and advancing homegrown industry.

The Green Upheaval, sent off during the 1960s and 1970s, was a huge achievement in India's post-freedom vision. It presented high-yielding harvest assortments, current horticultural practices, and the utilization of manures and pesticides to support food creation. The Green Upset assumed a significant part in accomplishing food security and expanding farming efficiency.

The modern area additionally saw significant development, with an accentuation on open area drove advancement. The Hindustan Machine Devices (HMT), Bharat Weighty Electricals Restricted (BHEL), and other public area undertakings assumed an essential part in India's industrialization. These undertakings pointed toward building an independent modern base that could take care of the country's developing requests.

The vision of industrialization reached out to the improvement of weighty enterprises, like steel, coal, and hardware. The Bhilai Steel Plant, dispatched in 1959, was one of the famous images of this work. It denoted India's obligation to building areas of strength for an establishment that could uphold the nation's development and improvement.

Urbanization and framework improvement were necessary parts of the post-freedom vision. The foundation of new urban communities, like Chandigarh and Bhubaneswar, and the improvement of arranged metropolitan regions mirrored a longing for present day metropolitan places. The development of an organization of thruways, dams, and extensions pointed toward further developing transportation and network.

The post-autonomy vision likewise looked to address civil rights and imbalance. India's chiefs were profoundly mindful of the need to change verifiable shameful acts and enable minimized networks. The booking framework, which distributed an extent of government occupations and instructive chances to Planned Standings, Booked Clans, and Other In reverse Classes, was acquainted with advance social consideration and equivalent open doors.

The obligation to civil rights stretched out to the annihilation of distance and the advancement of schooling among underestimated networks. Drives, for example, the foundation of the Public Planned Ranks Money and Advancement Partnership and the Booked Clans and Other Conventional Woods Inhabitants (Acknowledgment of Timberland Freedoms) Act meant to safeguard the privileges and government assistance of these networks.

In the field of training, the post-autonomy vision accentuated the significance of information and scholarly development. The foundation of the Indian Organizations of Innovation (IITs), Indian Establishments of The board (IIMs), and the development of colleges and exploration establishments were pointed toward advancing greatness in schooling and examination.

The post-autonomy vision additionally perceived the job of science and innovation in country building. Pioneers like Homi Bhabha and Vikram Sarabhai assumed a crucial part in propelling India's atomic and space programs. The effective send off of Aryabhata, India's most memorable satellite, in 1975, denoted the country's entrance into the field of room investigation.

India's post-freedom international strategy was molded by a guarantee to non-arrangement and serene concurrence. The nation tried to keep up with its sway and seek after its improvement objectives without arrangement with any significant power coalition. The Uncommitted Development (NAM), established in 1961, gave a stage to India to state its freedom and promoter for worldwide harmony and demilitarization.

The vision of post-freedom India reached out to its social and imaginative articulations. The nation commended its assorted social legacy through music, dance, writing, and the visual expressions. India's entertainment world, famously known as Bollywood, arose as a huge social peculiarity with a worldwide following.

While the post-autonomy vision was set apart by momentous accomplishments and goals, it was not without challenges. The course of financial preparation and state-drove improvement confronted analysis for its shortcomings and administration. The failures in the public area and the absence of a serious confidential area were viewed as obstacles to financial development.

The Green Transformation, while effective in expanding food creation, had ecological and social outcomes. The extreme utilization of compound composts and pesticides prompted soil corruption and natural contamination. Also, the advantages of the Green Unrest were not fairly appropriated, and differences in land proprietorship endured.

The obligation to confidence and protectionist arrangements, albeit planned to advance homegrown industry, on occasion smothered development and restricted admittance to worldwide business sectors. It prompted an absence of seriousness in certain ventures and made failures underway.

The booking framework, while pointed toward advancing civil rights, additionally confronted difficulties connected with its execution. There were worries about switch separation, and inquiries concerning the adequacy of the framework in resolving the more extensive issues of neediness and social imbalance.

The time of the 1990s denoted a defining moment in India's monetary vision. Financial advancement and globalization approaches, frequently alluded to as the New Monetary Arrangement, were presented. These strategies pointed toward opening up the Indian economy to unfamiliar venture, decreasing exchange hindrances, and empowering the confidential area.

The advancement period prompted huge changes in India's monetary scene. It worked with the development of the data innovation and programming administrations area, situating India as a worldwide center point for innovation and re-appropriating. The progress of Indian IT organizations, like Goodbye Consultancy Administrations (TCS) and Infosys, mirrored India's flexibility and seriousness in the worldwide market.

The post-progression period likewise considered the development of India to be a monetary force to be reckoned with. The country's development rates, albeit fluctuating, situated India as one of the world's quickest developing economies. The development of areas like broadcast communications, drugs, and sustainable power flagged another period of modern turn of events.

Urbanization and framework improvement proceeded, with the development of current urban areas, interstates, and air terminals. The public authority's "Make in India" drive, sent off in 2014, pointed toward advancing assembling and situating India as a worldwide assembling center.

The post-autonomy vision likewise tended to the significance of ecological manageability and sustainable power. The Public Activity Plan on Environmental Change, started in 2008, highlighted India's obligation to tending to environmental change and advancing clean energy arrangements.

The 21st century saw a change in India's international strategy and worldwide commitment. The nation produced vital organizations and assumed a huge part in global associations and gatherings. It expected to reinforce its situation on the worldwide stage and improve its political relations.

The post-autonomy vision for civil rights and consideration kept on advancing. India put forth attempts to advance orientation uniformity, with the entry of regulations and drives pointed toward safeguarding the privileges and security of ladies. The acquaintance of the Right with Instruction Act expected to give free and mandatory schooling to youngsters, facilitating the obligation to training for all.

The computerized insurgency and the far and wide utilization of cell phones and the web reshaped correspondence, network, and admittance to data. Drives like Computerized India planned to use innovation for administration, administration conveyance, and advanced strengthening.

In the social and imaginative circle, India's entertainment world proceeded to flourish and have a worldwide effect. Indian creators, performers, and craftsmen accomplished acknowledgment on the global stage, adding to the nation's delicate power and social tact.

2.1 The economic policies and strategies of post-independence India.

The financial approaches and techniques of post-autonomy India were figured out determined to cultivate monetary turn of events, independence, and civil rights. The heads of recently free India were confronted with the overwhelming undertaking of remaking the country's economy following quite a while of provincial rule. The monetary vision for post-freedom India was attached in a promise to accomplishing confidence, lessening neediness, and guaranteeing evenhanded circulation of assets.

One of the fundamental improvements in post-freedom India was the presentation of arranged monetary improvement through a progression of Five-Year Plans. The Initial Five-Year Plan, sent off in 1951, established the groundwork for an arranged and unified way to deal with financial development. These plans meant to address basic difficulties like food deficiencies, neediness, and joblessness.

The focal point of the Five-Year Plans was on accomplishing independence in key areas, especially in farming and industry. The horticultural area was designated through the Green Transformation, which presented high-yielding harvest assortments, current cultivating methods, and the utilization of composts and pesticides. These endeavors brought about a critical expansion in food creation, resolving issues of food security.

In the modern area, the plans underlined the improvement of center enterprises like steel, coal, and apparatus. The Bhilai Steel Plant, authorized in 1959, was symbolic of this procedure. Public area ventures like the Steel Authority of India Restricted (SAIL) and Bharat Weighty Electricals Restricted (BHEL) assumed a crucial part in this industrialization cycle.

The Second Five-Year Plan, sent off in 1956, proceeded with the accentuation on industrialization and the development of key areas. It likewise advanced the improvement of framework, for example, transportation organizations, power age, and media communications. These ventures were basic for supporting monetary development and cultivating advancement in different districts of the country.

The vision for monetary advancement stretched out past sectoral development to territorial turn of events and decreasing differences among states. The thought was to advance a reasonable financial improvement across various districts, guaranteeing that no single locale or state was abandoned. The arranging system incorporated the designation of assets, interest in foundation, and backing for neighborhood ventures.

The course of arranged improvement remembered a concentration for human resources. The post-autonomy pioneers perceived the significance of training, medical services, and abilities advancement in engaging the populace and advancing financial development. Drives like the foundation of the Indian Establishments of Innovation (IITs) and the development of instructive organizations planned to advance greatness in schooling and exploration.

The vision for post-autonomy India additionally incorporated the advancement of science and innovation. Pioneers like Homi Bhabha and Vikram Sarabhai assumed a huge part in propelling India's atomic and space programs. The effective send off of Aryabhata, India's most memorable satellite, in 1975, denoted the country's entrance into the field of room investigation.

While the arranged monetary improvement approach was instrumental in tending to a portion of India's difficulties, it likewise confronted reactions. Pundits contended that the cycle was administrative and wasteful, prompting defers in project execution and asset distribution. The emphasis on weighty businesses at times brought about lopsided characteristics in the advancement of various areas, dismissing the capability of more modest and medium-sized enterprises.

The protectionist strategies of post-freedom India were expected to advance independence and safeguard homegrown enterprises. Nonetheless, they likewise prompted an absence of seriousness in specific areas and restricted admittance to worldwide business sectors. The shut economy approach confined unfamiliar speculation and exchange, which hampered financial development and mechanical headways.

The financial arrangements of post-freedom India were additionally set apart by the state's critical job in monetary preparation and public area drove advancement. The public authority effectively settled and oversaw public area ventures in different enterprises, including steel, mining, energy, and media communications. The thought was to guarantee that key areas were under state control and could be utilized as instruments for arranged improvement.

The Green Unrest, while effective in expanding food creation, likewise had ecological and social outcomes. The broad utilization of compound composts and pesticides prompted soil corruption, ecological contamination, and wellbeing concerns. Moreover, the advantages of the Green Unrest were not evenhandedly conveyed, and differences in land proprietorship and admittance to assets endured.

The time of the 1990s denoted a critical change in India's monetary strategies. Financial advancement and globalization approaches, frequently alluded to as the New Monetary Strategy, were presented. These approaches pointed toward opening up the Indian economy to unfamiliar speculation, decreasing exchange hindrances, and empowering the confidential area.

The advancement time prompted significant changes in India's financial scene. It worked with the development of the data innovation and programming administrations area, situating India as a worldwide center point for innovation and rethinking. The outcome of Indian IT organizations, like Goodbye Consultancy Administrations (TCS) and Infosys, mirrored India's flexibility and seriousness in the worldwide market.

The monetary advancement arrangements additionally prompted the development of areas like media communications, drugs, and environmentally friendly power. Unfamiliar direct venture (FDI) assumed a vital part in supporting these enterprises. The drug business, specifically, saw critical development and became known as the "drug store of the world."

The post-progression period additionally saw the rise of India as a financial force to be reckoned with. The country's development rates, albeit fluctuating, situated India as one of the world's quickest developing economies. The development of little and medium-sized endeavors (SMEs) and the ascent of the administrations area added to India's financial dynamism.

Urbanization and framework improvement proceeded, with the development of current urban communities, interstates, and air terminals. The public authority's "Make in India" drive, sent off in 2014, pointed toward advancing assembling and situating India as a worldwide assembling center.

The progression strategies empowered the improvement of a serious confidential area, and India saw the development of business combinations, for example, the Goodbye Gathering, Dependence Enterprises, and the Aditya Birla Gathering. These combinations assumed a huge part in different areas, including broadcast communications, energy, and retail.

The New Financial Strategy likewise saw the presentation of the Protections and Trade Leading group of India (SEBI) to manage and foster the protections market. The securities exchange turned into an imperative part of India's monetary framework, drawing in speculations from homegrown and unfamiliar financial backers.

The change in India's monetary approaches stretched out to the monetary area. The progression strategies prompted the foundation of private banks, the improvement of a serious financial area, and the extension of administrations, for example, retail banking, Visas, and internet banking. These progressions further developed admittance to monetary administrations for the populace.

The job of innovation and development in India's financial vision is unquestionable. The "Advanced India" crusade, sent off in 2015, planned to tackle innovation for administration, administration conveyance, and computerized strengthening. Drives like "Aadhaar," a novel distinguishing proof framework, and the computerized installments framework assumed a huge part in monetary consideration and advanced change.

The post-freedom vision for India, the way things are today, is described by a concurrence of customary qualities and current desires. It envelops the quest for monetary development, innovative progressions, and worldwide commitment. India's obligation to a majority rules government, secularism, and social variety is key to its character.

In any case, the post-advancement time additionally wrestles with difficulties. Pay imbalance, ecological corruption, and provincial variations keep on being areas of concern. The sloppy area, which includes a huge piece of the labor force, frequently faces issues connected with employer stability, low wages, and absence of social security.

India's mission for comprehensive turn of events and impartial open doors stays a continuous excursion. Drives like "Swachh Bharat Abhiyan" (Clean India Mission) and "Ayushman Bharat" (Public Well-being Assurance Plan) mirror India's obligation to tending to disinfection and medical care difficulties.

The job of agribusiness in India's financial vision stays critical. In spite of the development of different areas, farming keeps on utilizing a huge part of the populace. Drives, for example, the Public Horticulture Market (eNAM) expect to work on rural showcasing and make a brought together public market for farming produce.

The nation's social and political texture is molded by complex issues connected with character, religion, and station. Tending to these intricacies, advancing social congruity, and guaranteeing that improvement helps all sections of society are continuous difficulties.

The post-autonomy monetary vision likewise stretches out to the worldwide stage. India's international strategy looks to cultivate monetary collaboration and key associations with different countries. The nation assumes a functioning part in worldwide associations and discussions, upholding for issues like environmental change, worldwide harmony, and manageable turn of events.

2.2 The promotion of heavy industries and self-sufficiency.

In the early long periods of post-autonomy India, the country's administration perceived the basic significance of advancing weighty ventures and accomplishing independence in different areas of the economy. This vision was attached in the longing to construct major areas of strength for a base, lessen reliance on imported products, and cultivate financial confidence. The advancement of weighty ventures assumed a urgent part in forming India's financial scene during this period.

One of the central components of this vision was the idea of independence. India had gotten through hundreds of years of pioneer rule, which had left the country financially helpless and intensely dependent on imports for key labor and products. Post-autonomy pioneers accepted that accomplishing independence was fundamental for secure the country's financial and political power.

The Initial Five-Year Plan, sent off in 1951, set up for arranged financial turn of events and the advancement of weighty businesses. The arrangement stressed the need to lay out a powerful modern base that could uphold the nation's developing requests. At its center, the arrangement planned to diminish India's reliance on imported products and encourage homegrown creation.

One of the huge drives during this period was the foundation of public area endeavors in key businesses. The public authority played a functioning job in making and overseeing state-claimed organizations, for example, the Steel Authority of India Restricted (SAIL), Bharat Weighty Electricals Restricted (BHEL), and Oil and Gaseous petrol Enterprise (ONGC). These endeavors were entrusted with the improvement of basic businesses like steel, power age, and oil investigation.

The advancement of weighty ventures, especially the steel business, assumed an imperative part in India's independence process. The Bhilai Steel Plant, dispatched in 1959, was an image of India's obligation to modern turn of events. It became one of the biggest and most mechanically progressed steel plants in the country.

The steel business was viewed as the foundation of modern development, giving unrefined components to different areas, including development, apparatus, and assembling. The foundation of steel plants intended to satisfy the developing needs of the framework and assembling areas, which were fundamental for financial turn of events.

One more key part of advancing weighty ventures was the advancement of foundation. The public authority perceived that a vigorous foundation was significant for supporting modern development and guaranteeing the productive transportation of merchandise and assets. Thus, huge speculations were made in the development of transportation organizations, including streets, rail routes, and ports.

The development of framework stretched out to the power area. The improvement of nuclear energy stations and hydropower projects planned to address the energy needs of the developing modern and metropolitan focuses. These undertakings were fundamental for supporting the apparatus and gear utilized in weighty ventures.

The Second Five-Year Plan, sent off in 1956, proceeded with the emphasis on industrialization and foundation advancement. It underscored the need to additionally extend key businesses and backing the development of the modern area. Moreover, it elevated local improvement to decrease differences among various states and areas.

The vision for weighty businesses was intently attached to making a confident India. The pioneers perceived that to accomplish independence, the country expected to foster its modern capacities and diminish its dependence on imported products. This approach was supported by the standards of financial patriotism and self-assurance.

While the advancement of weighty ventures and independence was instrumental in tending to the financial difficulties looked by post-freedom India, it was not without its portion of reactions and difficulties. Pundits contended that the emphasis on weighty businesses some of the time prompted irregular characteristics in the advancement of various areas. The disregard of more modest and medium-sized enterprises restricted the enhancement of the economy.

The protectionist arrangements that planned to safeguard home-grown enterprises from unfamiliar rivalry were viewed as boundaries to development and seriousness. The shut economy approach limited unfamiliar venture and exchange, which hampered financial development and innovative headways. The restricted admittance to worldwide business sectors impeded India's capacity to send out its items and create unfamiliar trade.

Regardless of the difficulties, the advancement of weighty enterprises lastingly affected India's modern scene. The steel business, specifically, kept on assuming a huge part in the nation's turn of events. The development of enterprises like coal, hardware, and power age added to India's financial independence.

The time of the 1990s denoted a huge defining moment in India's monetary strategies. Financial advancement and globalization strategies were presented, frequently alluded to as the New Monetary Strategy. These approaches pointed toward opening up the Indian economy to unfamiliar venture, diminishing exchange obstructions, and empowering the confidential area.

The progression period achieved massive changes in India's monetary scene. It worked with the development of the administrations area, especially the data innovation and programming administrations industry. This area situated India as a worldwide center for innovation, programming improvement, and reevaluating.

The progression arrangements additionally prompted the development of areas like media communications, drugs, and environmentally friendly power. Unfamiliar direct speculation (FDI) assumed a vital part in supporting these ventures. The drug business, specifically, experienced huge development and became known as the "drug store of the world."

The time of progression saw the development of business aggregates and the development of the confidential area. Business gatherings, for example, the Goodbye Gathering, Dependence Enterprises, and the Aditya Birla Gathering extended their tasks in different areas, including media communications, energy, and retail.

The progression arrangements likewise stretched out to the monetary area. The foundation of private banks, the advancement of a serious financial area, and the development of administrations, for example, retail banking, Mastercards, and web based banking further developed admittance to monetary administrations for the populace.

The securities exchange turned into a fundamental part of India's monetary framework. The Protections and Trade Leading body of India (SEBI) was laid out to direct and foster the protections market, drawing in speculations from homegrown and unfamiliar financial backers. The securities exchange arose as a huge road for venture and abundance creation.

The job of innovation and advancement in India's financial vision turned out to be progressively conspicuous during the progression time. The "Advanced India" crusade, sent off in 2015, expected to tackle innovation for administration, administration conveyance, and computerized strengthening. Drives, for example, "Aadhaar," a novel ID framework, and computerized installments frameworks assumed a critical part in monetary consideration and advanced change.

The advancement strategies additionally changed India's unfamiliar exchange and venture scene. The nation effectively looked for unfamiliar ventures, consented to exchange arrangements, and turned into a more necessary piece of the worldwide production network. India's commodity area, including data innovation, drugs, and administrations, saw critical development and worldwide intensity.

The progression period cultivated a culture of business venture and development. New businesses and innovation organizations started to multiply, adding to India's standing as a center for tech development and a prospering beginning up biological system.

The post-progression monetary scene addresses a takeoff from the previous spotlight on weighty enterprises and independence. While weighty ventures keep on assuming a urgent part, the economy is presently portrayed by a different scope of areas, including administrations, innovation, and information based businesses.

2.3 The rise of steel as a symbol of progress.

Steel, frequently alluded to as the foundation of industrialization, assumed an essential part in molding India's monetary scene during the post-freedom period. It arose as an image of progress, improvement, and independence, mirroring the country's obligation to building areas of strength for an establishment and diminishing its reliance on imported products. The ascent of the steel business was firmly interlaced with India's excursion towards accomplishing monetary sway and independence.

The Advancement of the Steel Business:

The advancement of the steel business was a focal component of India's post-freedom vision. The requirement for a strong steel industry was obvious, as steel is a principal unrefined substance expected for different areas, including development, hardware, assembling, and framework improvement. To guarantee financial independence, India expected to create its steel as opposed to depending on imports.

The Bhilai Steel Plant:

One of the most notable images of India's obligation to steel creation was the Bhilai Steel Plant, dispatched in 1959. Situated in the province of Chhattisgarh, Bhilai Steel Plant was a cutting edge office that obvious a critical achievement in India's modern turn of events. It was planned with the help of the Soviet Association and addressed an agreeable mix of Indian and Soviet designing mastery.

Bhilai Steel Plant was a steel creation office as well as a municipality intended to oblige the plant's labor force. The plant was outfitted with trend setting innovations for steelmaking, including impact heaters, moving factories, and other related foundation. It assumed a significant part in helping steel creation in India and supporting different modern areas.

Independence and Monetary Sway:

The foundation of Bhilai Steel Plant and other steel creation offices mirrored India's assurance to accomplish independence. The capacity to deliver its steel implied that India was presently not dependent on imported products for a significant natural substance. This was a huge step towards decreasing monetary weakness and guaranteeing independence.

The steel business was viewed as a critical driver of modern development. Steel is fundamental for the development of framework, hardware, and an extensive variety of purchaser products. By advancing the steel business, India intended to make areas of strength for a for industrialization and monetary turn of events.

Lessening Reliance on Imports:

Preceding autonomy, India was intensely subject to imported steel, essentially from the Unified Realm and the US. This reliance had serious financial and political ramifications. By fostering its steel industry, India expected to decrease its dependence on imported products, guaranteeing that the country's financial advantages were no longer helpless before worldwide business sectors.

The foundation of Bhilai Steel Plant and other steel offices implied that India could deliver steel locally, fulfilling the developing needs of its modern and framework projects. This essentially diminished the requirement for exorbitant imports and reinforced the country's monetary independence.

Advancement of Local Turn of events:

The advancement of weighty businesses like steel additionally added to local turn of events. The foundation of Bhilai Steel Plant, for example, changed the area of Chhattisgarh. The plant gave work open doors as well as prompted the development of another modern town. This model was recreated in different pieces of the nation, advancing the objective of adjusted territorial turn of events.

Improvement of Associated Businesses:

The development of the steel business affected different areas. Partnered ventures like mining, transportation, and assembling experienced huge development. The steel business required a consistent stock of unrefined substances, including iron metal and coal, which prompted the improvement of mining tasks in districts wealthy in these assets.

Transportation networks likewise saw improvement to work with the development of natural substances and completed steel items. The development of assembling enterprises was driven by the interest for hardware and gear utilized in the steel creation process.

Difficulties and Reactions:

While the advancement of the steel business was instrumental in accomplishing independence and lessening reliance on imports, it additionally confronted difficulties and reactions. Pundits contended that the emphasis on weighty businesses at times brought about uneven characters in the advancement of various areas. The disregard of more modest and medium-sized ventures restricted the enhancement of the economy.

The protectionist arrangements that intended to safeguard home-grown enterprises from unfamiliar contest were viewed as obstructions to development and seriousness. The shut economy approach confined unfamiliar speculation and exchange, which hampered monetary development and mechanical progressions. The restricted admittance to worldwide business sectors frustrated India's capacity to send out its items and produce unfamiliar trade.

Also, the steel business, as other weighty enterprises, had natural outcomes. The creation cycle produced outflows, and the mining of natural substances affected the climate. Throughout the long term, there was a developing familiarity with the requirement for manageable and harmless to the ecosystem rehearses in weighty businesses.

The Period of Monetary Progression:

The time of the 1990s denoted a critical defining moment in India's monetary strategies. Financial advancement and globalization strategies, frequently alluded to as the New Monetary Arrangement, were presented. These approaches pointed toward opening up the Indian economy to unfamiliar venture, diminishing exchange hindrances, and empowering the confidential area.

The advancement period achieved tremendous changes in India's financial scene. It worked with the development of the administrations area, especially the data innovation and programming administrations industry. This area situated India as a worldwide center point for innovation, programming improvement, and reevaluating.

The progression strategies additionally prompted the extension of areas like media communications, drugs, and sustainable power. Unfamiliar direct venture (FDI) assumed an essential part in supporting these businesses. The drug business, specifically, experienced huge development and became known as the "drug store of the world."

The change in India's monetary strategies reached out to the monetary area. The foundation of private banks, the improvement of a cutthroat financial area, and the extension of administrations, for example, retail banking, Visas, and internet banking further developed admittance to monetary administrations for the populace.

The securities exchange turned into an indispensable part of India's monetary framework. The Protections and Trade Leading group of India (SEBI) was laid out to control and foster the protections market, drawing in speculations from homegrown and unfamiliar financial backers. The securities exchange arose as a huge road for venture and abundance creation.

The Job of Innovation and Development:

The time of progression cultivated a culture of business venture and development. New businesses and innovation organizations started to multiply, adding to India's standing as a center point for tech development and a thriving beginning up biological system. The country's progress in data innovation and programming administrations was especially significant.

The job of innovation and development in India's monetary vision turned out to be progressively noticeable. The "Computerized India" crusade, sent off in 2015, meant to bridle innovation for administration, administration conveyance, and advanced strengthening. Drives, for example, "Aadhaar," a novel distinguishing proof framework, and computerized installments frameworks assumed a huge part in monetary consideration and computerized change.

The steel business, which had once represented independence and weighty industrialization, additionally went through changes during this period. While it stayed a basic area for foundation and development, the emphasis on innovation and administrations became the dominant focal point in India's monetary development.

The Advancement of India's Financial Scene:

The development of India's monetary scene mirrors the progress from an emphasis on weighty enterprises, represented by the ascent of steel, to a more different and administration situated economy. While the steel business keeps on being a vital part of India's modern structure, the country's monetary development is described by many areas, including data innovation, drugs, media communications, and sustainable power.

Chapter 3

"Forging a Nation"

The excursion of producing a country is a perplexing and multi-layered one, especially with regards to a different and old human progress like India. The post-freedom time frame in India's set of experiences saw the exhausting errand of uniting a country from a place that is known for some dialects, religions, societies, and customs. This cycle was set apart by political, social, and financial changes, as well as huge difficulties that India needed to defeat in its mission to turn into a unified and prosperous country.

Political Unification and Division:

At the core of India's excursion to nationhood was the course of political unification. India was a place that is known for royal states and districts under English pilgrim rule, and subsequent to acquiring freedom in 1947, the test was to bring these different elements under a solitary political umbrella. The heads of the time, including Mahatma Gandhi, Jawaharlal Nehru, Sardar Patel, and others, embraced the great undertaking of incorporating these regal states into a bound together country. Sardar Vallabhbhai Patel, specifically, assumed a vital part in persuading and haggling with the regal states to join the recently framed Indian Association.

The mix of royal states and the outlining of the Indian Constitution in 1950 established the groundwork for India's majority rule and government structure. The constitution cherished standards of secularism, a majority rules government, and the security of individual freedoms, setting the structure for a unified and various country. It additionally recognized the significance of etymological and social variety by perceiving various dialects and societies inside the Indian Association.

Be that as it may, the political unification of India was joined by huge difficulties. The parcel of India in 1947, which prompted the making of Pakistan, brought about enormous movements and common savagery. The scars of parcel and its effect on India's political and social texture are as yet felt today. India's political excursion has additionally been set apart by provincial desires, etymological developments, and requests for statehood and independence, prompting the revamping of states along semantic lines.

The Job of Secularism and A majority rules government:

Secularism and a majority rules government were the core values that formed India's country building process. The possibility of a common state was revered in the Indian Constitution, which ensured strict opportunity and equivalent treatment to all residents, regardless of their confidence. India's obligation to secularism was a reaction to its strict and social variety, as the country is home to different religions, including Hinduism, Islam, Christianity, Sikhism, Buddhism, and others.

India's popularity based framework was one more pivotal part of fashioning a country. The nation embraced a parliamentary majority rule government, with ordinary decisions at both the state and public levels. This framework gave a stage to different voices and permitted residents to take part in the political cycle. The occasional exchange of force through races turned into a sign of Indian majority rules government.

The meaning of these standards was obvious in India's capacity to oblige and commend its variety. While there have been difficulties connected with common pressures and strict struggles, India's obligation to secularism and a vote based system has stayed a relentless anchor in its country building venture.

Social Combination and Difficulties:

Social combination was a crucial part of manufacturing a country, given India's different populace with different ranks, networks, and ethnic gatherings. The post-autonomy time frame saw endeavors to address social abberations, elevate minimized networks, and advance civil rights. The Indian Constitution remembered arrangements for governmental policy regarding minorities in society through bookings for schooling and government occupations for Planned Positions, Planned Clans, and Other In reverse Classes.

Social change developments, drove by pioneers like B.R. Ambedkar and Periyar E.V. Ramasamy, pointed toward testing age-old acts of standing segregation and unapproachability. These developments looked to make a more comprehensive and libertarian culture. The battle for the privileges of ladies and orientation equity additionally picked up speed during this period.

While huge headway has been made in advancing civil rights and consideration, challenges endure. Issues connected with standing segregation, orientation imbalance, and social biases keep on influencing different sections of society. India's excursion toward social incorporation is a continuous one, and the country keeps on wrestling with these perplexing issues.

Financial Turn of events and Confidence:

Monetary turn of events and confidence were basic parts of India's country building process. The nation had acquired a pilgrim economy that was vigorously situated towards serving the interests of the English Realm. Present freedom India looked for on outline its own financial way and decrease its reliance on unfamiliar powers.

The time of arranged financial turn of events, started through the Five-Year Plans, pointed toward tending to basic difficulties like food deficiencies, neediness, and joblessness. These plans underlined the advancement of key areas, including farming, industry, and foundation. The Green Unrest, for example, presented high-yielding harvest assortments, current cultivating procedures, and the utilization of composts and pesticides to increment food creation.

In the modern area, the advancement of weighty businesses, like steel and power age, was a huge part of monetary turn of events. Public area ventures assumed an essential part in this cycle. The Bhilai Steel Plant, authorized in 1959, represented India's obligation to modern development and independence.

The advancement of confidence and diminishing reliance on imported products was another critical monetary system. India tried to locally make areas of strength for a base, empowering the creation of fundamental products. The improvement of native innovations and the extension of innovative work foundations were essential to this vision.

Nonetheless, the monetary approaches of post-freedom India likewise confronted reactions. Pundits contended that the course of arranged advancement was in many cases regulatory and wasteful, prompting defers in project execution and asset portion. The protectionist arrangements restricted admittance to worldwide business sectors and unfamiliar venture, frustrating monetary development and innovative progressions.

The monetary scene changed during the 1990s with the presentation of financial progression and globalization strategies. These strategies opened up the Indian economy to unfamiliar speculation, diminished exchange hindrances, and supported the confidential area. This shift prompted huge changes in India's financial design, cultivating the development of areas like data innovation, broadcast communications, drugs, and administrations.

India's excursion toward financial turn of events and confidence is progressing. While the nation has taken huge steps in different areas, challenges connected with pay imbalance, natural corruption, and provincial variations remain. The country keeps on making progress toward comprehensive development and evenhanded open doors for every one of its residents.

Social Variety and Public Personality:

Social variety has been a characterizing element of India's country building process. The nation is home to a bunch of dialects, religions, customs, and social practices. The Constitution of India perceives this variety and ensures social and instructive privileges to minority networks.

The post-autonomy time frame saw endeavors to advance and protect India's rich social legacy. Drives to secure and advance different dialects, old style expressions, and old customs were embraced. The All India Radio (AIR) and Doordarshan, India's public broadcasting company, assumed a critical part in spreading social substance to a wide crowd.

India's entertainment world, frequently alluded to as Bollywood, flourished during this period and had a worldwide effect. Indian creators, performers, and craftsmen accomplished acknowledgment on the worldwide stage, adding to the nation's delicate power and social tact.

Public character was likewise molded by the upsides of a majority rules system, secularism, and a promise to pluralism. The Preface to the Indian Constitution mirrors these qualities and accentuates equity, freedom, equity, and organization. While the nation has confronted difficulties connected with shared pressures and strict contentions, these qualities keep on being at the center of India's public character.

International strategy and Worldwide Commitment:

India's international strategy and worldwide commitment play had a critical impact in its country building venture. The nation embraced a strategy of non-arrangement during the Virus War, trying to keep up with its sway and freedom by not lining up with either the Western or Eastern coalitions. India assumed a functioning part in the Uncommitted Development (NAM) and upheld for worldwide harmony and demobilization.

Throughout the long term, India has constructed vital organizations and collusions with different nations. The country effectively takes part in worldwide associations and discussions, resolving worldwide issues, for example, environmental change, reasonable turn of events, and peacekeeping. India's international strategy mirrors its obligation to a multipolar world and the advancement of its monetary and security interests.

3.1 A closer look at the steel industry's growth and development.

The steel business possesses a focal situation in the story of India's industrialization and financial turn of events. As one of the key areas liable for the country's development, the steel business' process has been set apart by critical achievements, challenges, and extraordinary minutes that have added to India's independence and infrastructural progress. In this investigation, we will investigate the development and improvement of the steel business in post-freedom India.

The Introduction of Bhilai Steel Plant:

One of the pivotal occasions as India continued looking for independence and industrialization was the foundation of the Bhilai Steel Plant in 1959. This notable office, situated in the territory of Chhattisgarh, arose as an image of India's obligation to steel creation and weighty industry. Bhilai Steel Plant was planned and set up with specialized help from the Soviet Association, denoting a joint effort between two countries.

At the core of the plant's creation was the vision of accomplishing confidence in steel creation. Preceding autonomy, India had been vigorously subject to steel imports, essentially from the Unified Realm and the US. The foundation of Bhilai Steel Plant was a huge step towards decreasing this reliance and getting the country's monetary power.

The Bhilai Steel Plant became one of the biggest and most mechanically progressed steel plants in India, furnished with impact heaters, moving factories, and related foundation. Its essential area close to rich wellsprings of unrefined substances, like iron mineral and coal, assumed a crucial part in the outcome of the plant.

The Job of the Steel Business in Financial Turn of events:

The steel business' importance goes past its job as a maker of a key unrefined substance. Steel is a flexible material utilized in different areas, including development, hardware, assembling, and framework improvement. Accordingly, the development of the steel business was basic in supporting and impelling the development of different ventures and the general economy.

The foundation of Bhilai Steel Plant and other steel creation offices addressed a promise to building a powerful modern base. This base was fundamental for understanding India's vision of independence and lessening reliance on imported products. The development of native steel creation not just addressed the necessities of India's modern and framework projects yet additionally added to a decrease in the requirement for expensive steel imports.

The steel business likewise assumed a crucial part in supporting the improvement of other unified enterprises. Digging tasks for iron metal and coal, both basic unrefined substances for steel creation, extended to guarantee a consistent stockpile. Transportation organizations, including railroads and streets, were created to work with the development of unrefined components and completed steel items. This, thus, prompted the development of the transportation and coordinated factors areas.

Moreover, the development of the steel business created critical interest for apparatus and gear. This request gave force to the assembling area, adding to India's more extensive industrialization and independence objectives. The steel business, with its flowing consequences for united ventures, turned into a key part of India's financial improvement system.

Difficulties and Reactions:

While the advancement of the steel business and weighty ventures overall was instrumental in accomplishing independence and decreasing reliance on imports, it was not without its portion of reactions and difficulties. Pundits contended that the emphasis on weighty businesses in some cases prompted irregular characteristics in the advancement of various areas. The disregard of more modest and medium-sized enterprises restricted the broadening of the economy.

The protectionist strategies that expected to safeguard homegrown enterprises from unfamiliar rivalry were additionally viewed as hindrances to advancement and intensity. The shut economy approach, which limited unfamiliar speculation and exchange, ruined financial development and innovative progressions. The restricted admittance to worldwide business sectors shortened India's capacity to send out its items and produce unfamiliar trade.

Natural worries were one more issue related with the steel business and other weighty enterprises. The creation cycle, especially in the early years, produced huge discharges and affected the climate. Over the long haul, there was a developing acknowledgment of the requirement for manageable and harmless to the ecosystem rehearses in weighty businesses.

The Period of Financial Advancement:

The time of the 1990s denoted a critical defining moment in India's financial strategies. Monetary advancement and globalization arrangements were presented, frequently alluded to as the New Financial Approach. These arrangements pointed toward opening up the Indian economy to unfamiliar speculation, decreasing exchange obstructions, and empowering the confidential area.

The advancement period achieved massive changes in India's monetary scene. It worked with the development of the administrations area, especially in data innovation and programming administrations. This area situated India as a worldwide center point for innovation, programming improvement, and re-appropriating. The product business, frequently alluded to as the IT blast, pulled in huge unfamiliar speculations and made India a worldwide innovation player.

The advancement approaches likewise prompted the development of areas like broadcast communications, drugs, and sustainable power. Unfamiliar direct venture (FDI) assumed a critical part in supporting these enterprises. The drug business, specifically, experienced critical development and became known as the "drug store of the world."

The change in India's monetary approaches stretched out to the monetary area. The foundation of private banks, the improvement of a cutthroat financial area, and the extension of administrations, for example, retail banking, Mastercards, and web based banking further developed admittance to monetary administrations for the populace. The securities exchange turned into an essential part of India's monetary framework.

The Protections and Trade Leading body of India (SEBI) was laid out to manage and foster the protections market, drawing in speculations from homegrown and unfamiliar financial backers. The securities exchange arose as a huge road for venture and abundance creation. The job of innovation and development in India's monetary vision turned out to be progressively noticeable during the advancement time.

The Changing Scene of India's Steel Industry:

The advancement strategies changed the scene of India's steel industry. While it stayed a critical area for foundation and development, the emphasis on innovation and administrations became the overwhelming focus in India's monetary development. The development of businesses like data innovation, media communications, drugs, and administrations flagged a change in the country's financial needs.

India's steel industry additionally went through changes during this period. New innovations and cycles were taken on to upgrade effectiveness and lessen natural effect. The business kept on satisfying the needs of foundation and development, yet it was additionally expected to adjust to the advancing monetary scene.

3.2 Profiles of pioneering entrepreneurs and industrialists.

India's excursion towards financial turn of events and industrialization owes a lot to the vision and persistence of spearheading business people and industrialists who assumed a urgent part in molding the country's monetary scene. These people showed an interesting mix of development, risk-taking, and assurance, contributing essentially to

India's independence and worldwide intensity. In this investigation, we will dive into the profiles of a portion of these wonderful figures who made a permanent imprint on India's modern history.

Jamsetji Goodbye (1839-1904):

Jamsetji Goodbye, frequently alluded to as the "Father of Indian Industry," was a visionary business person and giver who established the groundwork for the Goodbye Gathering, one of India's biggest and most regarded business combinations. Brought into the world in a group of Parsi clerics, Jamsetji Goodbye showed early indications of enterprising soul. His determined quest for industrialization and country building made him a vital figure in India's modern history.

In 1868, Jamsetji established the Goodbye Gathering, which at first centered around materials. Be that as it may, his vision stretched out past materials to different areas basic for India's turn of events. He imagined a steel plant to diminish India's reliance on steel imports. His fantasy emerged with the foundation of the Goodbye Iron and Steel Organization (TISCO) in 1907, three years after his passing.

TISCO's steel plant in Jamshedpur was India's previously coordinated steel plant, denoting a huge step towards independence in steel creation. The plant assumed a fundamental part in giving natural substances to India's foundation improvement and assembling areas.

Jamsetji Goodbye's vision reached out past business. He was a donor who put stock in rewarding society. He established foundations like the Indian Organization of Science (IISc) in Bangalore and the Goodbye Establishment of Sociologies (TISS) to advance training and exploration. The Goodbye Gathering keeps on maintaining his tradition of magnanimity and corporate social obligation.

J.R.D. Goodbye (1904-1993):

Jamsetji Goodbye's inheritance was conveyed forward by his nephew, Jehangir Ratanji Dadabhoy Goodbye, all the more ordinarily known as J.R.D. Goodbye. J.R.D. Goodbye was a spearheading industrialist, pilot, and humanitarian who took the Goodbye Gathering higher than ever.

Under his authority, the Goodbye Gathering enhanced into different enterprises, including avionics, steel, autos, and cordiality. Goodbye Engines, Goodbye Consultancy Administrations (TCS), and Goodbye Tea (presently Goodbye Purchaser Items) are among the outstanding organizations that were laid out or extended during his residency. He was likewise instrumental in the foundation of Air India, India's most memorable global carrier.

J.R.D. Goodbye's commitments reached out to the social and altruistic circles also. He assumed an essential part in the improvement of the Goodbye Remembrance Medical clinic for malignant growth therapy and the Goodbye Foundation of Crucial Exploration (TIFR) for logical examination. His obligation to social causes, flying, and business greatness acquired him various honors and honors, including the Bharat Ratna, India's most elevated non military personnel grant.

Dhirubhai Ambani (1932-2002):

Dhirubhai Ambani, the organizer behind Dependence Ventures, was a quintessential independent business person whose poverty to newfound wealth venture has turned into the stuff of legend in India's business history. Brought into the world in a humble family in Gujarat, Dhirubhai's excursion from a little exchanging business to laying out one of India's biggest combinations is a demonstration of his business sharpness, risk-taking capacity, and vision.

In 1958, he established Dependence Business Company, which later changed into Dependence Ventures. Dhirubhai's vision was to make India confident in material assembling. Under his authority, Dependence Enterprises ventured into assorted areas, including petrochemicals, refining, broadcast communications, and retail.

One of his most critical commitments was in making India independent in polyester producing. His creative techniques, remembering in reverse coordination and a concentration for vertical development, reshaped India's material and petrochemical industry. Dependence's development in the petrochemical area situated India as a worldwide player in the business.

Dhirubhai Ambani was known for his allure and capacity to draw in financial backers and investors. His spearheading endeavors in value gathering pledges and the democratization of possession through Dependence's Underlying Public Contributions (Initial public offerings) became industry benchmarks.

His innovative excursion was not without discussion and legitimate difficulties, but rather his effect on India's financial scene is certain. Dhirubhai Ambani's heritage lives on through his children, Mukesh and Anil Ambani, who have proceeded to grow and differentiate the Dependence Gathering.

N.R. Narayana Murthy (b. 1946):

Nagavara Ramarao Narayana Murthy, the fellow benefactor of Infosys, is a spearheading figure in India's data innovation and programming administrations industry. Brought into the world in Mysore, Karnataka, N.R. Narayana Murthy's enterprising excursion is pull in his energy for innovation and a dream to put India on the worldwide IT map.

In 1981, Narayana Murthy and six fellow benefactors began Infosys with a simple $250 in capital. The organization at first gave programming administrations and framework incorporation arrangements. In any case, what put Infosys aside was its obligation to quality, moral strategic policies, and a worldwide viewpoint. These qualities turned into the foundations of the organization's way of life.

Under his authority, Infosys developed to become one of the world's driving IT administrations organizations. Narayana Murthy's accentuation on development, client centricity, and a straightforward corporate administration system situated Infosys as a worldwide IT arrangements supplier.

He likewise assumed a huge part in upholding for India's innovation industry and was instrumental in molding the country's IT strategies. Infosys' prosperity prepared for the development of India's IT and programming administrations area, adding to the country's standing as a worldwide innovation center point.

Narayana Murthy's commitments stretch out past business. He has been engaged with charitable drives and has pushed for corporate social obligation. His administration and values keep on affecting India's innovation area and act as a motivation for trying business visionaries.

Adi Godrej (b. 1942):

Adi Godrej is the director of the Godrej Gathering, a noticeable Indian combination with interests in different areas, including shopper merchandise, land, and horticulture. Under his initiative, the Godrej Gathering has extended its impression both inside India and around the world.

Adi Godrej's innovative excursion started with his family's locks and safes business. He extended the organization's item portfolio to incorporate customer merchandise, machines, and land. The Godrej Gathering's obligation to quality and development in customer items made it an easily recognized name in India.

The gathering's introduction to land improvement added to India's urbanization and foundation development. The foundation of Godrej Properties Restricted flagged the gathering's obligation to feasible and harmless to the ecosystem development rehearses.

Adi Godrej's commitments to Indian business and business have procured him various honors and acknowledgments. His vision, obligation to morals, and spotlight on manageability lastingly affect the Godrej Gathering and India's business scene.

Kiran Mazumdar-Shaw (b. 1953):

Kiran Mazumdar-Shaw, the organizer and director of Biocon Restricted, is a spearheading figure in India's biotechnology and drug industry. Her innovative excursion is portrayed by breaking orientation boundaries and making huge commitments to the field of life sciences.

In 1978, Kiran Mazumdar-Shaw established Biocon, at first as a joint endeavor with an Irish firm. The organization's emphasis on innovative work in biotechnology prompted notable advancements in medical care. Biocon turned into a worldwide player in biopharmaceuticals, especially in regions like insulin and monoclonal antibodies.

Mazumdar-Shaw's enterprising excursion was not without challenges. She confronted wariness and obstructions because of her orientation in a male-ruled industry. Her diligence and obligation to science and development prompted Biocon's development and acknowledgment as one of India's driving biotech organizations.

Her commitments to biotechnology and medical care in India have procured her various honors and respects. Kiran Mazumdar-Shaw's process mirrors her commitment to development, business venture, and the headway of the biopharmaceutical area in India.

3.3 Technological advancements and production milestones.

The excursion of India's industrialization and financial improvement has been set apart by critical innovative headways and creation achievements. These achievements are characteristic of the country's advancement in different areas, including assembling, agribusiness, and administrations. In this investigation, we will investigate a portion of the vital mechanical headways and creation achievements that have molded India's financial scene.

Green Upheaval and Horticultural Change:

One of the main creation achievements in India's set of experiences was the Green Upheaval, a time of fast horticultural change that started during the 1960s. The Green Upheaval was portrayed by the reception of high-yielding harvest assortments, current cultivating procedures, and the utilization of manures and pesticides to increment food creation.

The impetus for this change was the turn of events and dispersal of high-yielding wheat and rice assortments. These new yield assortments, frequently alluded to as marvel seeds, were stronger, sickness safe, and had a more limited development cycle. They altogether expanded crop yields, especially in states like Punjab and Haryana.

The Green Transformation prompted a significant expansion in food creation, making India independent in food grains and diminishing its reliance on imports. It assumed a urgent part in tending to food deficiencies and starvation, guaranteeing food security for the developing populace. The innovation driven way to deal with farming was a significant step in the right direction in modernizing India's horticultural area.

Space Exploration and Satellite Innovation:

India's space exploration and satellite innovation have been instrumental in a large number of uses, from correspondence and remote detecting to weather conditions determining and public safety. The Indian Space Exploration Association (ISRO) has been at the front of these headways.

India's process in space research started with the send off of its most memorable satellite, Aryabhata, in 1975. From that point forward, ISRO has accomplished various creation achievements, including sending off in excess of 300 satellites into space for different purposes. The fruitful Mars Orbiter Mission (Mangalyaan) in 2013 and the Chandrayaan missions to the Moon have situated India as a central participant in planetary investigation.

The advancement of the Polar Satellite Send off Vehicle (PSLV) and the Geosynchronous Satellite Send off Vehicle (GSLV) has permitted India to send off satellites for both homegrown and global clients. These send-offs play had a critical impact in upgrading India's correspondence framework and remote detecting capacities.

India's space innovation has tracked down applications in farming, calamity the executives, route, and asset the board. Remote detecting satellites have empowered better harvest observing and the executives, prompting expanded rural efficiency. The innovation has likewise been essential in anticipating catastrophic events and aiding fiasco the board endeavors.

IT and Programming Administrations:

The development of India's data innovation (IT) and programming administrations area has been quite possibly of the most extraordinary mechanical headway in late many years. This area has reshaped the worldwide business scene and situated India as a center for innovation, programming improvement, and rethinking.

The IT and programming administrations area took off during the 1990s, with pioneers like Infosys, Wipro, and Goodbye Consultancy Administrations (TCS) driving the way. These organizations gave programming arrangements and administrations to worldwide clients, becoming central parts in the worldwide IT industry.

India's gifted labor force, capability in the English language, and financially savvy administrations made it an alluring objective for IT re-appropriating. The area made great many positions and contributed fundamentally to India's monetary development.

The development of the IT area has additionally prompted the foundation of innovation parks and unique monetary zones (SEZs) devoted to IT and programming administrations. These center points house IT organizations, support administrations, and foundation, cultivating development and mechanical progressions.

Drug Industry and Medication Assembling:

The drug business in India has taken huge steps in drug assembling and advancement. India has become known as the "drug store of the world" because of its job in delivering reasonable conventional medications and antibodies for different sicknesses.

The drug area saw achievements like the foundation of the Indian Drug Affiliation (IPA) in 1939 and the advancement of the Medication Value Control Request in 1970 to manage drug costs. These drives intended to guarantee admittance to fundamental meds for the Indian populace.

India's drug industry plays had a vital impact in giving conventional meds to treat sicknesses like HIV/Helps, jungle fever, and tuberculosis, making medical services more open in India and different nations. The business' abilities in innovative work (Research and development) and assembling have extended to fulfill global quality guidelines.

The presentation of the Exchange Related Parts of Licensed innovation Privileges (Outings) Understanding in 1995 denoted a critical achievement for India's drug industry. It expected India to change its patent regulations, which prompted expanded advancement and interest in Research and development. India's drug organizations began fostering their protected medications and biosimilars, growing their worldwide reach.

Broadcast communications and Portable Transformation:

The broadcast communications area has seen a mechanical upheaval in India, especially with the coming of cell phones and remote correspondence. The development of this area has been portrayed by expanded availability, reasonableness, and broad reception of versatile innovation.

The progression of the telecom area in the mid 1990s denoted a critical achievement, prompting the passage of private players and contest in the business. The state-possessed Bharat Sanchar Nigam Restricted (BSNL) confronted rivalry from organizations like Bharti Airtel, Vodafone (presently converged with Thought), and Dependence Jio.

The presentation of portable administrations and the extension of the telecom foundation assumed a vital part in expanding network in country and metropolitan regions. The development of cell phone utilization added to monetary consideration and admittance to computerized administrations, changing the manner in which individuals convey and get to data.

The send off of Dependence Jio in 2016 disturbed the telecom market by offering reasonable information and voice administrations. This prompted expanded information utilization, cell phone reception, and the multiplication of advanced administrations, including portable banking, internet business, and content web based.

Sustainable power and Sun oriented Power:

India's quest for perfect and economical energy sources has seen striking mechanical progressions in the field of sustainable power, especially sunlight based power. India's Public Sunlight based Mission, sent off in 2010, expected to advance sun oriented energy and lessen ozone depleting substance discharges.

India's sunlight based power limit has developed fundamentally, with achievements like the charging of the Charanka Sun oriented Park in Gujarat, perhaps of the biggest sun based park in Asia. The recreation area houses various sun powered projects and has an all out limit of more than 2,000 MW.

The improvement of sun based power innovation and sunlight powered charger producing has added to India's obligation to decrease its carbon impression. The expense of sunlight based power has diminished, making it a financially savvy and practical energy source.

Thermal power and Power Age:

India's thermal power program has accomplished critical mechanical headways in power age. The nation's excursion in thermal power started with the foundation of the Goodbye Organization of Major Exploration (TIFR) and the Nuclear Energy Commission (AEC) during the 1940s.

India's most memorable atomic reactor, Apsara, went basic in 1956, denoting a critical achievement in atomic innovation. The country's most memorable business thermal energy station, Tarapur Nuclear Power Station, was authorized in 1969.

India's obligation to quiet purposes of thermal power for power age has prompted the advancement of Compressed Weighty Water Reactors (PHWRs) and Light Water Reactors (LWRs). The presentation of the Indo-U.S. common atomic arrangement in 2008 denoted a significant improvement in India's thermal power program, considering global participation in atomic innovation and exchange.

Chapter 4

"Balancing Growth and Responsibility"

The financial direction of any country is portrayed by the quest for development, advancement, and flourishing. India, with its assorted and dynamic economy, is no exemption for this standard. Throughout the long term, the nation has taken huge steps in different areas, adding to its development as one of the world's quickest developing significant economies. Nonetheless, the quest for monetary development frequently accompanies a bunch of liabilities and difficulties. Adjusting the goals of development with social and ecological obligation is a sensitive errand that India has been exploring as it propels on its formative process.

Financial Development and Its Effects:

Financial development is an essential objective for any country looking to increase the living expectations of its residents and address issues of neediness and disparity. For India's situation, the quest for financial development was a basic following its freedom in 1947. The nation was confronted with the gigantic test of elevating a huge populace from neediness and tending to the horde financial differences that existed.

The excursion of financial development in India was set apart by a progression of monetary strategies and changes, especially during the post-freedom time frame. The early years saw an accentuation on state-drove arranging and public area predominance. Five-year plans were figured out to direct monetary turn of events and industrialization.

The Modern Approach Goal of 1956 and the foundation of public area endeavors (PSUs) were a portion of the critical achievements in forming India's modern scene. The accentuation was on building an independent economy, with an emphasis on weighty businesses and framework improvement.

The time of the 1990s saw a huge change in financial strategy with the commencement of monetary progression and globalization. Changes pointed toward lessening exchange hindrances, opening up the economy to unfamiliar venture, and advancing the confidential area. These progressions prompted a flood in monetary development, especially in areas like data innovation, media communications, and administrations.

India's development story earned worldwide respect, and the nation arose as a key part in the worldwide economy. The development in per capita pay, extension of the working class, and expanded admittance to training and medical care addressed huge accomplishments. Nonetheless, the quest for financial development likewise delivered a bunch of difficulties that required cautious thought.

Difficulties of Comprehensive Development:

The test of accomplishing comprehensive development, where the advantages of financial improvement are shared by an expansive range of the populace, was a focal concern. India's financial advancement had prompted a noticeable decrease in destitution, however pay disparity endured. There were variations in pay, schooling, medical care, and admittance to fundamental administrations.

Horticulture, notwithstanding being a significant supporter of work, stayed set apart by low efficiency, lacking foundation, and agrarian trouble. The metropolitan provincial gap as far as pay and valuable open doors kept on being a major problem.

The nation confronted a double test of tending to the requirements of an expanding youthful populace while guaranteeing that the advantages of development arrived at underestimated networks and districts. Accomplishing comprehensive development expected designated approaches and mediations to connect financial holes and give equivalent open doors to all.

Ecological Obligation and Manageability:

As India's monetary development flooded, concerns in regards to its effect on the climate and regular assets came to the front. The quest for industrialization, foundation improvement, and urbanization had ramifications for land use, air and water quality, and the generally speaking environmental equilibrium.

Ecological difficulties included issues like air contamination, deforestation, water shortage, and the consumption of normal assets. The unfriendly impacts of environmental change, with expanded occurrences of outrageous climate occasions, further highlighted the significance of ecological obligation.

India recognized the need to address these difficulties and embraced a multi-pronged way to deal with ecological maintainability. Drives like the Public Clean Air Program (NCAP) expected to battle air contamination, while the Green India Mission zeroed in on afforestation and biodiversity preservation.

India additionally dedicated to its job in worldwide endeavors to battle environmental change, as reflected in its promise to decrease fossil fuel byproducts as a component of the Paris Understanding. The advancement of environmentally friendly power sources like sun based and wind power assumed an imperative part in moderating the country's carbon impression.

Social Obligation and Human Turn of events:

The quest for financial development should be joined by a guarantee to social obligation, with an emphasis on human improvement markers.

Schooling, medical care, and social government assistance are basic parts of this obligation.

India's excursion towards social obligation saw the execution of different arrangements and projects pointed toward upgrading human turn of events. The Right to Schooling Act, passed in 2009, ordered free and necessary training for all youngsters up to the age of 14. The Public Wellbeing Mission, sent off in 2013, planned to further develop medical care framework and administrations.

Social government assistance programs like the Mahatma Gandhi Public Rustic Work Assurance Act (MGNREGA) gave business open doors and federal retirement aide to country populaces. The Pradhan Mantri Jan Dhan Yojana (PMJDY) tried to advance monetary consideration by guaranteeing admittance to banking administrations for all.

Be that as it may, while these drives were significant positive developments, there remained difficulties with regards to quality and access. Abberations in training, medical care, and pay kept on enduring, especially in provincial and distant regions.

The Job of Innovation and Advancement:

Innovation and development play had a critical impact in tending to the difficulties of development and obligation. India's product administrations area, frequently alluded to as the IT blast, was a spearheading force in utilizing innovation for monetary turn of events. The area worked with computerized change, empowered e-administration, and extended admittance to data and administrations.

Advancements in medical care, for example, telemedicine and portable wellbeing applications, further developed admittance to clinical benefits, especially in country regions. Portable banking and monetary innovation assumed a fundamental part in upgrading monetary consideration.

The Swachh Bharat Abhiyan, or Clean India Mission, tackled innovation to address sterilization and cleanliness issues. The reception of e-administration and computerized stages smoothed out managerial cycles and decreased debasement.

Corporate Social Obligation (CSR):

The idea of Corporate Social Obligation (CSR) acquired noticeable quality as a method for organizations to add to social and ecological prosperity. The Organizations Act, 2013, ordered that specific organizations dispense a part of their benefits towards CSR exercises.

CSR drives incorporated many exercises, including training, medical care, natural preservation, and local area improvement. Organizations put resources into projects pointed toward engaging networks and advancing supportability.

CSR endeavors likewise stretched out to supporting abilities advancement and business among oppressed populaces. By adjusting business targets to social and ecological obligations, organizations tried to make a positive effect on society.

Foundation Advancement and Network:

Foundation improvement assumed a vital part in adjusting development and obligation. Interest in transportation, energy, and computerized foundation further developed availability and worked with financial development.

The Pradhan Mantri Gram Sadak Yojana (PMGSY) planned to give all-climate street availability to country regions, decreasing separation and empowering admittance to business sectors and administrations. The improvement of parkways and interstates upgraded intercity availability and exchange.

Interest in energy foundation, especially in the sustainable power area, meant to diminish fossil fuel byproducts and give admittance to clean energy sources. The extension of computerized framework, including the BharatNet project, looked to connect the advanced separation and further develop admittance to data and online administrations.

The Job of Schooling and Ability Improvement:

Training and expertise advancement have been integral to accomplishing capable development. The Public Expertise Improvement Mission intended to give professional preparation and ability advancement amazing chances to upgrade employability.

Notwithstanding essential and optional training, professional and specialized schooling programs were significant in setting up the labor force for a quickly developing position market. Drives like Expertise India meant to engage people with the abilities expected to succeed in various businesses.

Local area Strengthening and Grassroots Drives:

Local area based programs and grassroots drives assumed a crucial part in advancing mindful development. Self improvement gatherings, microfinance foundations, and local area driven advancement projects engaged people and networks to assume responsibility for their financial prosperity.

Programs like the Public Rustic Work Mission (NRLM) upheld the development of self improvement gatherings and gave admittance to credit and vocation amazing open doors. These drives encouraged business venture, confidence, and social incorporation.

Challenges and the Way Forward:

Adjusting development and obligation is a continuous excursion for India. Difficulties like pay imbalance, natural debasement, and differences in admittance to training and medical services keep on presenting complex issues.

Tending to these difficulties requires a multi-layered approach that consolidates strategy changes, mechanical developments, and a promise to maintainability and social government assistance. It likewise requests an emphasis on rustic turn of events, comprehensive .

4.1 The environmental and social implications of rapid industrialization.

Quick industrialization, driven by the development of assembling and modern areas, has been a characterizing component of many creating economies, including India. This cycle is portrayed by the change of agrarian social orders into modern forces to be reckoned with, with an emphasis on weighty enterprises, framework improvement, and urbanization. While quick industrialization offers various monetary open doors and advantages, it likewise achieves critical natural and social ramifications that should be painstakingly made due. In this investigation, we will dig into the complicated transaction of industrialization with its ecological and social outcomes, with a specific spotlight on the Indian setting.

Natural Ramifications:

Air Contamination and Respiratory Wellbeing: Quick industrialization frequently prompts expanded discharges of toxins into the environment. The consuming of petroleum products, modern cycles, and vehicular discharges add to elevated degrees of air contamination. The wellbeing outcomes are serious, as unfortunate air quality is connected to respiratory infections, like asthma and constant obstructive pneumonic sickness (COPD), as well as cardiovascular issues.

Water Contamination and Tainting: Industrialization is a critical wellspring of water contamination. Processing plants release untreated effluents into streams and water bodies, prompting pollution and hurting sea-going life. Synthetic overflow from modern regions can likewise invade groundwater, influencing the drinking water supply and prompting a large group of medical problems, including waterborne sicknesses.

Soil Corruption and Land Use Changes: Quick industrialization can bring about land use changes, including the transformation of horticultural land for modern purposes. This can prompt soil corruption and loss of arable land. Besides, modern exercises might include the utilization of dangerous synthetic compounds that can saturate the dirt, making it barren and influencing crop efficiency.

Deforestation and Natural surroundings Misfortune: The requirement for assets to fuel modern development frequently prompts deforestation, which has huge ecological ramifications.

Deforestation disturbs biological systems, lessens biodiversity, and adds to environmental change by delivering carbon dioxide put away in trees. This deficiency of territory likewise compromises many plant and creature species.

Environmental Change and Ozone depleting substance Emanations: Fast industrialization is related with expanded ozone harming substance discharges. The consuming of petroleum derivatives for energy creation, transportation, and modern cycles discharges carbon dioxide, methane, and other ozone depleting substances into the air, adding to an Earth-wide temperature boost and environmental change. India, as one of the world's biggest carbon producers, faces the test of lessening discharges while supporting monetary development.

Squander Age and The executives: The development of businesses prompts expanded squander age. Ill-advised removal of modern waste can bring about landfills and dumps that are unsafe to both the climate and human wellbeing. Successful waste administration and reusing frameworks are crucial to relieve the natural effects of waste.

Regular Asset Consumption: Fast industrialization frequently puts gigantic tension on normal assets like minerals, water, and energy. Impractical asset extraction and usage can prompt their consumption, influencing the climate as well as the drawn out maintainability of businesses.

Social Ramifications:

Dislodging and Urbanization: Quick industrialization is regularly joined by urbanization, with country populaces moving to urban communities looking for better business amazing open doors. This metropolitan movement can prompt the relocation of networks from their conventional grounds and homes, bringing about friendly disturbance and frequently lacking everyday environments in metropolitan ghettos.

Work Double-dealing and Working Circumstances: chasing modern development, work serious ventures frequently utilize a huge labor force. Be that as it may, abuse of work, unfortunate working circumstances, low wages, and absence of employer stability can be inescapable issues. Guaranteeing fair wages, safe work environments, and laborers' freedoms is fundamental for social supportability.

Pay Imbalance: Quick industrialization can fuel pay disparity as the advantages of monetary development are not equally dispersed all of the time. While certain sections of society benefit from industrialization through work and venture open doors, underestimated networks may not encounter critical upgrades in that frame of mind of living.

Wellbeing Effects: The natural outcomes of industrialization can have direct wellbeing suggestions. Air and water contamination, as well as openness to perilous materials, can prompt different medical problems, including respiratory infections, waterborne ailments, and long haul medical conditions, excessively influencing weak populaces.

Social and Social Disturbance: The fast speed of industrialization can upset customary ways of life, social practices, and local area bonds. As individuals move to metropolitan regions, the social texture of provincial networks can be stressed, prompting a feeling of misfortune and separation.

Orientation Variations: Ladies frequently endure the worst part of social ramifications, confronting extraordinary difficulties in getting to training, medical care, and financial open doors. Orientation differences can be exacerbated in industrialized locales on the off chance that even-handed approaches are not set up.

Framework Advancement: While industrialization might prompt better foundation like streets, power, and medical services offices, these improvements are not uniformly disseminated 100% of the time. Provincial regions might fall behind metropolitan habitats, prompting a country metropolitan improvement partition.

Asset Clashes: Fast industrialization can increase clashes over assets, like water, land, and minerals. This can bring about land questions, removal, and social agitation.

Techniques for Alleviation and Reasonable Industrialization:

Offsetting quick industrialization with natural and social obligation requires an exhaustive methodology that tends to the difficulties while bridling the potential open doors for development. A few techniques can add to relieving the unfortunate results of industrialization:

Ecological Guidelines and Implementation: Severe natural guidelines, alongside compelling requirement, are pivotal to control emanations, oversee squander, and safeguard normal assets. Ventures ought to stick to outflow norms, execute squander the executives rehearses, and participate in reasonable asset the board.

Interest in Clean Advances: Empowering enterprises to take on cleaner advances and feasible practices is fundamental. Interests in sustainable power, energy effectiveness, and eco-accommodating assembling cycles can lessen natural effects.

Natural Effect Evaluations: Directing careful ecological effect appraisals prior to starting modern ventures can assist with distinguishing likely ecological perils and propose relief measures.

Asset Proficiency: Advancing asset effectiveness in ventures, including productive utilization of natural substances, energy, and water, can decrease ecological pressure and improve manageability.

Green Framework: Creating green foundation, like metropolitan parks, green rooftops, and afforestation programs, can relieve the natural effects of quick urbanization and industrialization.

Social Wellbeing Nets: Laying out friendly security nets, including government assistance projects and medical care administrations, can moderate the social ramifications of industrialization by offering help to minimized and weak populaces.

Work Changes: Guaranteeing fair work rehearses, sensible wages, and safe working circumstances is fundamental to safeguard the freedoms and prosperity of laborers in modern settings.

Local area Commitment: Including neighborhood networks in the dynamic cycle and guaranteeing that they benefit from modern undertakings can assist with resolving issues connected with relocation and social disturbance.

Ability Improvement and Schooling: Putting resources into training and expertise advancement projects can engage the labor force and upgrade their employability in arising modern areas.

Orientation Uniformity and Social Incorporation: Strategies that advance orientation correspondence, social consideration, and fair dissemination of advantages from industrialization are fundamental for a more adjusted and just society.

4.2 Sustainability and responsible industrial practices.

Maintainability and mindful modern practices have arisen as basic goals for countries and enterprises around the world. The quick speed of industrialization and financial development has required a change in context, stressing the significance of long haul natural, social, and monetary supportability. In this investigation, we will dive into the meaning of maintainability and mindful modern practices, their standards, and their suggestions for ventures and society.

Figuring out Maintainability:

Manageability is the ability to persevere or keep up with crucial natural, financial, and social frameworks after some time. It is many times portrayed as the convergence of three key aspects:

Ecological Manageability: This aspect centers around the capable use and preservation of normal assets, lessening waste and contamination, and safeguarding biological systems. It involves guaranteeing that modern exercises don't exhaust assets quicker than they can be normally recharged and that they don't make hopeless harm the climate.

Monetary Manageability: Financial supportability underscores long haul monetary development, dependability, and thriving without compromising the government assistance of people in the future. It requires a reasonable way to deal with monetary improvement that guarantees monetary security, admittance to assets, and open doors for all.

Social Supportability: Social manageability frets about the prosperity of people and networks, resolving issues like equity, civil rights, common liberties, and the safeguarding of social personalities. It looks to guarantee that modern practices advance the wellbeing and personal satisfaction of current and people in the future.

Supportability is generally about addressing the necessities of the present without compromising the capacity of people in the future to address their own issues. With regards to modern practices, supportability makes an interpretation of into a guarantee to diminishing natural effects, further developing asset effectiveness, maintaining moral work guidelines, and contributing decidedly to the networks wherein ventures work.

Standards of Capable Modern Practices:

Mindful modern practices are established in the standards of supportability. These standards guide the manner in which businesses work, simply decide, and collaborate with the climate and society. Some center standards of dependable modern practices include:

Asset Productivity: Ventures ought to intend to utilize assets, like energy, water, and natural substances, as productively as could really be expected. This limits squander, decreases creation costs, and diminishes ecological effects.

Natural Stewardship: Capable enterprises are focused on ecological preservation and stewardship. They carry out practices to lessen contamination, limit their carbon impression, and safeguard normal environments and biodiversity.

Straightforwardness: Straightforwardness is vital to capable modern practices. Enterprises ought to give precise and available data about their tasks, ecological effects, and social drives. This straightforwardness encourages trust among partners, including clients, financial backers, and networks.

Consistence with Guidelines: Ventures should comply to every single pertinent regulation and guidelines connected with natural security, work freedoms, and wellbeing norms. Consistence is the groundwork of capable tasks.

Moral Work Practices: Capable ventures treat their representatives decently, give safe working circumstances, and advance variety and consideration in the work environment. Work practices ought to maintain common liberties and work norms.

Local area Commitment: Businesses draw in with neighborhood networks and partners to comprehend their requirements, address concerns, and add to nearby turn of events. This incorporates supporting schooling, medical services, and social drives in the areas where they work.

Advancement and Persistent Improvement: Mindful businesses are focused on development and nonstop improvement. They put resources into innovative work to track down additional economical advances and practices that diminish ecological effects.

Round Economy: Embracing the standards of the roundabout economy, businesses intend to decrease squander by planning items and cycles that empower reuse, reusing, and negligible asset exhaustion.

Reasonable Advancement Objectives (SDGs):

The Unified Countries' Reasonable Improvement Objectives (SDGs) give a worldwide structure to tending to squeezing worldwide difficulties, including neediness, imbalance, environmental change, natural corruption, harmony, and equity. The 17 SDGs and their 169 targets set explicit goals to be accomplished by 2030. Capable modern practices line up with a few of these objectives, including:

SDG 7: Reasonable and Clean Energy: Empowering the utilization of environmentally friendly power sources and further developing energy proficiency in modern cycles.

SDG 8: Good Work and Financial Development: Advancing moral work rehearses, work creation, and fair wages in the modern area.

SDG 9: Industry, Development, and Framework: Putting resources into maintainable foundation, mechanical advancement, and mindful industrialization.

SDG 12: Mindful Utilization and Creation: Empowering dependable asset use, squander decrease, and maintainable creation and utilization designs.

SDG 13: Environment Activity: Diminishing fossil fuel byproducts, supporting environment relief and transformation gauges, and changing to low-carbon modern practices.

SDG 15: Life Ashore: Safeguarding biological systems and biodiversity by limiting the ecological effect of modern exercises.

Ecological Effects and Alleviation:

Capable modern practices address different natural difficulties by limiting the adverse consequences of modern exercises and advancing asset protection. A few critical natural effects and relief measures include:

Air Contamination: Businesses can lessen air contamination by taking on cleaner advances, utilizing discharges control frameworks, and sticking to emanation principles. Endeavors to progress to sustainable power sources likewise add to bring down fossil fuel byproducts.

Water Contamination: Treating and overseeing modern wastewater before release into water bodies can assist with decreasing water contamination. Capable ventures carry out productive water use practices and utilize green framework for stormwater the board.

Asset Exhaustion: To alleviate the consumption of regular assets, ventures can zero in on asset proficiency and reusing. This incorporates planning items for toughness, diminishing waste, and putting resources into the roundabout economy.

Deforestation: Capable businesses resolve to zero-deforestation rehearses. They try not to source materials from deforested regions, advance reforestation, and backing feasible woods the executives.

Environmental Change: Alleviating environmental change requires decreasing ozone harming substance outflows. Ventures can accomplish this by utilizing cleaner energy sources, taking on energy-proficient innovations, and setting clear outflow decrease targets.

Social Effects and Responsiveness:

Mindful modern practices stretch out to social effects, guaranteeing that businesses maintain moral work principles, support networks, and advance social prosperity. Key social effects and responsive measures include:

Work Abuse: Mindful businesses pay fair wages, guarantee safe working circumstances, and give amazing open doors to ability improvement and profession development. They additionally restrict kid work and constrained work.

Local area Commitment: Ventures draw in with neighborhood networks to grasp their requirements and concerns. This incorporates supporting training, medical care, and social drives that upgrade the prosperity of local area individuals.

Orientation Correspondence: Dependable enterprises advance orientation equity by giving equivalent open doors, tending to wage differences, and offering family-accommodating arrangements that help balance between fun and serious activities.

Social Conservation: Businesses working in socially different regions ought to regard and support nearby societies and legacy. This incorporates drives to save social practices and backing native networks.

Social Obligation: Capable businesses put resources into social obligation programs, like medical services centers, instructive grants, and local area advancement projects. These drives assist with working on the personal satisfaction for those living close to modern offices.

Corporate Social Obligation (CSR):

Corporate Social Obligation (CSR) is a basic part of mindful modern practices. It includes organizations willfully making moves that benefit society past their center financial targets. CSR drives frequently envelop ecological assurance, moral work rehearses, local area commitment, and generous endeavors.

CSR programs add to cultural prosperity as well as improve an organization's standing, form client trust, and draw in moral financial backers. These drives might include supporting neighborhood schools, giving clean drinking water to networks, or leading reforestation projects. CSR is a way for enterprises to show their obligation to mindful and reasonable practices.

Difficulties and Hindrances:

While the standards of manageability and capable modern practices are broadly perceived, a few difficulties and boundaries might block their reception:

Transient Benefit Thought process: Ventures might focus on momentary benefits over long haul manageability because of tension from investors and financial backers. Accomplishing a harmony between quick monetary benefits and maintainability goals is urgent.

Asset Shortage: Enterprises frequently depend on limited assets, for example, minerals and metals, which might become more difficult to find over the long run. This can present difficulties to asset productive practices and require the advancement of elective materials and innovations.

4.3 Government policies and industry initiatives to address challenges.

The difficulties presented by quick industrialization, including ecological corruption, social disparities, and financial lopsided characteristics, require a cooperative exertion including government strategies and industry drives. These difficulties are mind boggling and multi-layered, requiring a blend of administrative structures, motivating forces, and intentional activities to accomplish supportable turn of events. In this investigation, we will analyze the job of government approaches and industry drives in tending to the difficulties related with industrialization.

Government Approaches:

Government strategies assume a focal part in molding the structure inside which businesses work. These strategies can either empower or block maintainable practices and should address the natural, social, and financial parts of industrialization.

Ecological Guidelines: Legislatures lay out natural guidelines to restrict and control the emanations and contamination produced by businesses. These guidelines set principles for air and water quality, garbage removal, and the assurance of normal territories.

Consistence with these guidelines is compulsory for ventures, and rebelliousness might bring about fines or authorizes. For example, the Spotless Air Act and the Perfect Water Act in the US are critical bits of regulation controlling air and water quality.

Emanation Decrease Targets: Numerous state run administrations have set aggressive focuses for lessening ozone harming substance outflows as a component of their endeavors to battle environmental change. These objectives urge businesses to embrace cleaner advances, decrease fossil fuel byproducts, and change to environmentally friendly power sources. The European Association's obligation to accomplishing carbon nonpartisanship by 2050 is an illustration of a thorough outflows decrease target.

Asset The board: To address asset consumption and deforestation, states might execute arrangements that advance maintainable asset the executives. This incorporates guidelines to forestall unlawful logging, implement economical timberland rehearses, and support capable asset extraction. The Timberland Stewardship Chamber (FSC) certificate is a worldwide drive that advances dependable backwoods the executives.

Environmentally friendly power Backing: States can give impetuses and appropriations to the reception of environmentally friendly power sources. This help incorporates tax breaks, feed-in levies, and monetary motivating forces to urge enterprises to progress to clean energy. Germany's Energiewende (energy progress) strategy is a noticeable instance of supporting the development of sustainable power sources.

Green Acquirement Strategies: States can show others how its done through green obtainment arrangements that favor harmless to the ecosystem items and administrations. These approaches animate interest for reasonable items and set out market open doors for businesses that take on eco-accommodating practices.

Social Obligation Drives: Arrangements advancing social obligation might zero in on work privileges, orientation equity, and local area commitment. Regulations can expect enterprises to maintain fair work rehearses, restrict kid work, and guarantee orientation balance in the working environment. The Fair Work Norms Act in the US, for example, sets compensation and hour guidelines.

Local area Advancement: Government arrangements can boost ventures to put resources into local area improvement drives. For instance, the Corporate Social Obligation (CSR) order in India requires specific organizations to designate a piece of their benefits to help projects that benefit neighborhood networks.

Instruction and Preparing: Legislatures can work with schooling and preparing projects to improve labor force abilities and advance supportability. Preparing programs for workers in ventures taking on green practices can encourage advancement and work on functional effectiveness.

Tax assessment and Motivating forces: Tax collection arrangements can be utilized to support manageable practices. Charge impetuses for energy-productive advances, reusing projects, and carbon decrease drives can rouse enterprises to put resources into manageability.

Partner Commitment: Legislatures can command or urge businesses to draw in with partners, including neighborhood networks, in dynamic cycles. This approach cultivates straightforwardness and empowers neighborhood voices to straightforwardly be heard in issues that influence them.

Industry Drives:

While government strategies set the general system, enterprises themselves play a basic part to play in embracing and supporting dependable practices. Industry drives are deliberate moves initiated by organizations to upgrade their obligation to manageability and address the difficulties presented by quick industrialization.

Corporate Social Obligation (CSR): Numerous ventures have taken on CSR drives to advance social obligation and moral strategic approaches. This incorporates supporting local area projects, giving representative advantages, and sticking to fair work guidelines. For example, the dress organization Patagonia is known for its obligation to natural and social obligation.

Economical Store network The board: Ventures can do whatever it takes to guarantee that their stock chains stick to supportability standards. This includes mindful obtaining of materials, moral work rehearses, and the decrease of waste in the store network. Organizations like Apple have carried out feasible inventory network drives to address natural and social worries.

Roundabout Economy Practices: The idea of the round economy includes diminishing, reusing, and reusing assets to limit squander and advance manageability. Enterprises can take on roundabout economy rehearses by planning items for life span, reusing materials, and diminishing the ecological effect of their tasks. The Ellen MacArthur Establishment advances the round economy idea around the world.

Eco-Accommodating Development: Ventures can drive advancement in eco-accommodating advances and practices. For example, car organizations are putting resources into electric vehicle innovation and advancing the reception of electric vehicles to lessen outflows and dependence on non-renewable energy sources.

Green Structure and Design: The development business can embrace green structure and engineering rehearses, which center around energy productivity, economical materials, and decreased natural effect. The Initiative in Energy and Natural Plan (LEED) certificate is a notable drive in the field.

Dependable Horticultural Practices: Enterprises connected with agribusiness can embrace maintainable cultivating rehearses, for example, natural cultivating, diminished pesticide use, and soil preservation strategies. These practices advance capable land use and safeguard environments.

Environmentally friendly power Ventures: Businesses can put resources into environmentally friendly power sources to decrease their carbon impression. Tech organizations like Google and Amazon have made significant interests in environmentally friendly power to control their activities.

Ecological Administration Frameworks (EMS): Executing EMS, for example, ISO 14001, assists industries with methodicallly overseeing and diminish their natural effect. These frameworks give a system to setting goals, observing execution, and constantly working on natural practices.

Industry Affiliations and Principles: Industry affiliations can assume a urgent part in setting and maintaining maintainability guidelines. For instance, the Practical Clothing Alliance (SAC) is an industry cooperation focused on further developing store network maintainability.

Accreditations and Names: Ventures can look for outsider certificates and marks that approve their adherence to maintainability and capable practices. Models incorporate Fair Exchange, Energy Star, and natural confirmations.

Difficulties and Contemplations:

In spite of the significance of government approaches and industry drives in tending to the difficulties of industrialization, there are a few difficulties and contemplations that should be considered:

Administrative Fluctuation: Guidelines and arrangements change across districts and nations, making it trying for ventures working internationally to explore varying consistence necessities. Fitting guidelines can advance supportability.

Intentional versus Compulsory Drives: While numerous enterprises willfully embrace maintainability drives, there might be calls for more noteworthy authorization of obligatory prerequisites to guarantee reliable reception of dependable practices.

Momentary versus Long haul Concentration: Ventures might focus on transient monetary profits over long haul maintainability targets. Adjusting the requirement for sure fire benefits with a guarantee to long haul supportability is fundamental.

Asset Requirements: Enterprises confronting asset shortage, like the minerals and metals area, may confront moves in progressing to reasonable practices. Putting resources into elective materials and advancements is vital.

Social and Work Issues: Tending to social and work issues, like orientation disparity and fair wages, can be intricate and require constant endeavors and observing.

Innovative Change: The progress to maintainable advancements and practices might include critical forthright expenses, which a few businesses might view as trying. Government motivators can assist with easing this weight.

Shopper Interest: The degree to which businesses take on manageability drives frequently relies upon buyer interest. Bringing issues to light and encouraging customer interest in maintainable items and practices is significant.

Estimating Effect: Estimating the effect of supportability drives and dependable practices can challenge. Creating normalized measurements for surveying natural and social effects is a continuous undertaking.

5

Chapter 5

"The Resilience of Steelworkers"

In the modern heartland of America, the steelworkers have for quite some time been the foundation of a country based on steel and sweat. Through financial expansions and busts, innovative upsets, and world-wide contest, these people have persevered, adjusting to the moving tides of their industry. Their flexibility is a demonstration of the strength of the human soul and the persevering through force of networks limited by mutual perspective.

The narrative of steelworkers is an account of perseverance, difficult work, and a profound association with the land they call home. For ages, they have worked in the steel factories, fashioning the unrefined components of current human advancement. A task requests actual strength, mental mettle, and an eagerness to overcome the cruelest of conditions. From the searing shoot heaters to the stunning thunder of the moving factories, steelworkers have confronted risks and difficulties that couple of different callings can coordinate.

However, notwithstanding the overwhelming idea of their work, steelworkers have shown an unflinching commitment to their art. They invest wholeheartedly in their capacity to create a material that is the foundation of endless businesses, from development to transportation to assembling. Steel, with its solidarity and flexibility, has been a foundation of progress and development for a really long time, and steelworkers play had an essential impact in molding the world as far as we might be concerned.

The steel business has forever been dependent upon the rhythmic movement of monetary powers. From the blast long stretches of post-war America to the difficult withdrawals of the 1970s and 80s, steelworkers have faced the hardships of financial vulnerability. They've confronted plant terminations, cutbacks, and compensation cuts, yet they've kept on appearing for work every day of, not set in stone to accommodate their families and backing their networks.

During seasons of emergency, the strength of steelworkers turns out to be considerably more clear. The Incomparable Downturn of 2008 managed a serious disaster for the American steel industry, prompting broad cutbacks and plant terminations. Many accepted that the times of the steelworker were numbered, as less expensive unfamiliar steel overflowed the market. Be that as it may, steelworkers, declining to be crushed, tracked down better approaches to adjust. They embraced advancement, modernizing their cycles and making their activities more effective. They additionally battled for fair exchange arrangements to shield American steel from out of line contest. Through their assurance and backing, they endure the emergency as well as aided lead the resurgence of the American steel industry.

The feeling of local area among steelworkers is a characterizing element of their calling. They frequently come from families with profound roots in the business, and the bonds framed on the plant floor run profound. Notwithstanding difficulty, this feeling of fortitude has been a wellspring of solidarity. At the point when one laborer is out of luck, their kindred steelworkers are there to help them. Whether it's getting sorted out food drives for battling families or pushing for more secure working circumstances, steelworkers pay special attention to each other.

The flexibility of steelworkers is likewise an impression of the networks they call home. Steel towns, with their very close areas and shared values, have been the foundation of the American steel industry. In places like Pittsburgh, Cleveland, and Gary, Indiana, the steel factory is something other than a position of work; it's an image of personality and pride. The neighborhood economies, schools, and social texture are profoundly entwined with the destiny of the steel business. At the point when the plants are flourishing, the entire local area benefits. At the point when challenges are out of hand, the whole town feels the effect.

Steelworkers have been at the front of endeavors to rejuvenate their networks. They comprehend that the destiny of the business and the prosperity of their towns are interlaced. They've been engaged with grassroots drives to draw in new organizations, put resources into training, and construct a broadened neighborhood economy. Their assurance to see their networks prosper is a demonstration of the profound feeling of obligation they feel towards their neighbors and the spots they call home.

The flexibility of steelworkers isn't simply an issue of individual courage and local area bonds; it's likewise a demonstration of their versatility and readiness to embrace change. The steel business has gone through huge changes throughout the long term. The times of old, when factories were boisterous, messy, and work serious, have given way to an all the more cutting edge and mechanized industry. Steelworkers have needed to master new abilities and adjust to new innovations, from PC controlled hardware to cutting edge metallurgy. They've shown a noteworthy ability to develop with the times, demonstrating that the familiar maxim "you can't impart new habits when old ones are so deeply ingrained" doesn't make a difference to them.

Perhaps of the main change in the steel business has been the shift towards an all the more earth manageable and energy-proficient model of creation. The customary picture of steel plants as contamination regurgitating monsters is being supplanted by a dream of cleaner, greener, and more proficient offices. Steelworkers play had a basic impact in this progress, embracing new innovations and practices that decrease the natural effect of their work. They comprehend that the fate of the business relies upon its capacity to adjust to the requests of an influencing world, and they are focused on being essential for the arrangement.

The steel business' flexibility is additionally attached to its capacity to face the hardships of global contest. In a globalized world, American steel should rival steel delivered in nations with lower work costs and different administrative principles. This has put huge strain on the homegrown business, prompting exchange debates and a consistent requirement for development and productivity. Steelworkers have not avoided this test; they've campaigned for fair exchange approaches and embraced the should be worldwide serious.

One of the vital turning points throughout the entire existence of American steel and the versatility of steelworkers came as an exchange question the mid 2000s. The business confronted a flood of modest steel imports, especially from China, which took steps to sabotage the homegrown market. Steelworkers and their associations assumed a urgent part in squeezing for exchange solutions for address this issue. The inconvenience of duties and standards helped even the odds and permitted American steel to recapture its balance.

The versatility of steelworkers isn't just about adjusting to change and confronting financial difficulties; it's likewise about defending their privileges and battling for a fair arrangement. Worker's guilds play had a crucial impact in addressing the interests of steelworkers and it are heard to guarantee that their voices. Through exchanges and once in a while strikes, steelworkers have gotten better wages, more secure working circumstances, and professional stability.

The connection among steelworkers and their associations is a complicated one. While associations have been instrumental in getting significant advantages for steelworkers, they've likewise confronted analysis and difficulties. A contend that associations can prompt firmness and higher work costs, possibly making American steel less serious. Others consider associations to be a fundamental offset to corporate power and a method for guaranteeing that laborers are dealt with reasonably.

Steelworkers have, on occasion, been trapped in these discussions, yet they've likewise shown an eagerness to work with their associations and the board to track down arrangements that benefit all gatherings. In doing as such, they've exemplified their obligation to everyone's benefit and their capacity to figure out something worth agreeing on even notwithstanding contrasting interests.

The eventual fate of the steel business is questionable, as it faces progressing difficulties, from the requirement for supportable practices to the consistently present apparition of worldwide contest. Steelworkers keep on adjusting, to enhance, and to battle for their industry and their networks. Not set in stone to keep the flames of the impact heater consuming and the steel plants murmuring.

The tale of the versatility of steelworkers is one of motivation. It's an account of networks meeting up, of people confronting difficulty with mental fortitude, and of an industry developing to fulfill the needs of an influencing world. A story helps us to remember the significance of difficult work, determination, and the force of human association. In a world that is continually changing, the flexibility of steelworkers fills in as a brilliant illustration of what can be accomplished when individuals meet up with a mutual perspective.

As we plan ahead, the illustrations of steelworkers are more important than any other time in recent memory. The difficulties confronting the steel business are reflected in numerous different areas of the economy. From assembling to energy creation, from horticulture to innovation, businesses are wrestling with the need to adjust to new real factors while guaranteeing the prosperity of their laborers and the maintainability of their practices.

The tale of the steelworker's flexibility advises us that the way ahead is generally difficult, however it is consistently conceivable. It requires devotion, development, and a pledge to figuring out some mutual interest. It likewise requires an acknowledgment that we are better off sticking together than going alone, that the prosperity of laborers and their networks is inherently connected to the progress of an industry.

In reality as we know it where innovation is quickly changing the idea of work and globalization is reshaping enterprises, the steelworker's story is an immortal one. It is an update that the upsides of difficult work, fortitude, and flexibility are persevering. These are the qualities that have permitted steelworkers to confront the difficulties of their time and arise more grounded. They are the qualities that can direct us as we stand up to the difficulties of our own time.

The flexibility of steelworkers isn't simply a verifiable artifact; it is a living demonstration of the getting through force of the American soul. It is an update that when we meet up, we can conquer even the most overwhelming difficulties.

5.1 The stories of workers and laborers in the steel industry.

The steel business, with its monumental plants, heaters, and production lines, has been a foundation of industrialization and progress for a really long time. Behind the monstrous hardware and the transcending smokestacks, there are the narratives of endless specialists and workers who have worked in the difficult and frequently unforgiving universe of steel creation. Their stories are a demonstration of the coarseness, assurance, and strength of the people who have formed the business and, thus, been molded by it.

In the beginning of the steel business, work was overwhelming and frequently risky. The steel factories of the nineteenth and mid twentieth hundreds of years were a long ways from the cutting edge, innovative offices of today. Laborers confronted brutal circumstances, extended periods, and the steady danger of mishaps. However, they endured, driven by a profound feeling of direction and the longing to accommodate their families.

One of the central attributes of steelworkers in these early years was their foreigner foundations. Large numbers of the people who worked in the steel factories came to the US looking for a superior life, and the steel business gave them open doors for business and an opportunity to construct a future. European foreigners, specifically, rushed to the steel towns of America, carrying with them their abilities, customs, and hard working attitude.

These foreigners were frequently exposed to unforgiving working circumstances. They persevered through outrageous intensity, poisonous exhaust, and the steady commotion of the plants. Wellbeing guidelines were frequently missing, and mishaps were very normal. However, these specialists, filled by their assurance and dreams of a more promising time to come, kept on working in the steel plants.

In numerous ways, the early steelworkers were pioneers, regarding industrialization as well as in fashioning a feeling of local area. They shaped affectionate areas in the towns encompassing the plants, making bonds that went past the working environment. These people group became blends of different societies, dialects, and customs, and the steel factories assumed a focal part in molding the character of these towns.

As the steel business developed and extended, so did the tales of its laborers. The modern upset achieved tremendous changes in innovation and creation strategies. The presentation of the Bessemer cycle and the open-hearth heater changed steel creation, making it more proficient and savvy. With these headways came new open doors for laborers, yet additionally new difficulties.

The steel business started to fill quickly in the late nineteenth and mid twentieth hundreds of years, encouraging a flood in interest for work. Steel plants extended, and new ones were inherent spots like Pittsburgh, Pennsylvania, and Gary, Indiana. The business turned into a significant financial power, attracting much more individuals to the steel towns. Laborers ended up laboring in ever-bigger offices, frequently with expanded motorization and a developing division of work.

The deluge of African American laborers into the steel business during the Incomparable Movement added a layer of variety to the labor force. They, as well, looked for better monetary open doors, leaving the isolated South for the modern North. In the steel factories, African American laborers confronted separation and inconsistent treatment.

Nonetheless, they persisted and contributed altogether to the business' development.

While steel offered open doors for financial progression, the existence of a steelworker was not without its difficulties. Laborers confronted genuinely requesting undertakings, extended periods of time, and the always present risk of mishaps. The steel factories worked nonstop, and shift work was normal. Laborers would get through outrageous intensity, vapor, and the consistent commotion of the plants, prompting medical problems and security concerns.

The tales of steelworkers are additionally set apart by the presence of worker's guilds. As the business developed and working circumstances stayed strenuous, laborers started to sort out and advocate for better treatment and pay. The development of worker's guilds in the steel business assumed a crucial part in getting the privileges and advantages of laborers. The Unified Steelworkers of America (USW) arose as a strong power, addressing the interests of steelworkers and haggling for their benefit.

The work development in the steel business was set apart by strikes and work debates. Laborers frequently took to the picket lines to request better wages, more secure working circumstances, and further developed benefits. These hits were frequently met with opposition from steel organizations, prompting conflicts that occasionally turned savage. The Estate Strike of 1892 and the Incomparable Steel Strike of 1919 are noticeable instances of these work clashes.

The narratives of steelworkers in the mid twentieth century are accounts of versatility and assurance. They confronted troublesome working circumstances, separation, and now and again fierce resistance to their requests. However, they kept on battling for their privileges and the advancement of their day to day routines and the existences of their families. Their battles helped make ready for the better circumstances and advantages delighted in by steelworkers today.

The mid-twentieth century carried further changes to the steel business, as innovation kept on progressing. The advancement of the essential oxygen process (BOP) and consistent projecting upset steelmaking, making it more proficient and financially savvy. These progressions fundamentally decreased the work power of steel creation, prompting shifts in the labor force.

The narratives of steelworkers from this period are set apart by the effect of innovation on their work. While mechanical progressions achieved more noteworthy proficiency and security enhancements, they additionally prompted changes in the workforce. The interest for specific ranges of abilities moved as a few customary positions were supplanted by machines and computerization.

The steel business' labor force turned out to be progressively particular, with laborers prepared to work and keep up with the high level apparatus. The requirement for talented professionals and specialists developed as the factories turned out to be more computerized. These progressions required a labor force that was versatile and ready to embrace new innovations.

The steel business' worker's guilds kept on assuming a critical part in upholding for the privileges and advantages of laborers. Aggregate haggling arrangements between the Unified Steelworkers of America and steel organizations turned into the norm for deciding wages, working circumstances, and advantages. Laborers accessed superior medical care, retirement plans, and employer stability through these discussions.

While the steel business experienced times of development and flourishing during the mid-twentieth hundred years, it likewise confronted difficulties from unfamiliar contest. Steel imports, especially from nations with lower work costs, represented a danger to the home-grown business. The narratives of steelworkers during this time are interlaced with endeavors to address these difficulties and guarantee the reasonability of American steel.

The 1970s and 1980s were especially difficult years for the American steel industry. A mix of variables, including worldwide rivalry and over-capacity, prompted a progression of plant terminations and cutbacks.

The deindustrialization of steel towns crushed networks, as laborers confronted joblessness and monetary difficulty.

The narratives of steelworkers during this period are set apart by their strength notwithstanding affliction. Laborers, their families, and whole networks were significantly impacted by the slump in the steel business. However, they wouldn't be crushed. Steelworkers, associations, and neighborhood pioneers mobilized together to track down arrangements and investigate new roads for renewing their towns.

Now and again, laborers partook in retraining projects to secure new abilities and change to different ventures. Neighborhood state run administrations and local area associations looked to expand the nearby economies, drawing in new organizations and ventures. These endeavors, while not without their difficulties, exhibited the assurance of steelworkers to adjust and revamp their networks.

One of the critical defining moments throughout the entire existence of the American steel industry and the accounts of its laborers came in the mid 2000s. The business confronted a flood of modest steel imports, especially from China, which took steps to sabotage the homegrown market. Steelworkers and their associations assumed a urgent part in squeezing for exchange solutions for address this issue. The inconvenience of taxes and quantities helped make everything fair and permitted American steel to recapture its balance.

The steelworkers' accounts from this period feature their support for fair exchange strategies and the significance of shielding homegrown enterprises from uncalled for contest. Their endeavors to address the difficulties of globalization displayed their flexibility and assurance to battle for their positions and networks.

As the 21st century advanced, the steel business kept on developing. The push for more noteworthy manageability and ecological obligation turned out to be progressively unmistakable. Steelmakers attempted to diminish their ecological impression by executing more proficient cycles and cleaner advancements. The tales of laborers in the steel business mirror their obligation to these progressions and their readiness to embrace new, more supportable practices.

The steel business of today is described by cutting edge innovation, computerization, and a solid spotlight on maintainability. Laborers in current steel plants work PC controlled apparatus and high level hardware. The business has likewise become all the more ecologically cognizant, with a promise to lessening emanations, reusing salvaged material, and preserving assets.

Steelworkers in the 21st century are exceptionally gifted and prepared experts. They have adjusted to the requests of an all the more cutting edge industry, embracing new innovations and cycles. The work might be less truly requesting than previously, yet it requires a profound comprehension of the hardware and materials utilized in steel creation.

5.2 Their contributions to India's industrial journey.

The modern excursion of India has been a complicated and dynamic one, set apart by hundreds of years of financial and mechanical change. At the core of this excursion are the innumerable people, networks, and ventures that have added to India's modern development. Their accounts uncover a rich embroidery of development, business, and flexibility, molding India's financial scene and character.

By and large, India has been known for its financial and modern ability. The Indus Valley Progress, going back more than 4,000 years, was one of the world's earliest urbanized social orders. It highlighted progressed metropolitan preparation, exchange, and businesses like earthenware and metalwork. This early human progress established the groundwork for India's modern process, exhibiting the country's antiquated pioneering soul.

India's commitments to industrialization took on new aspects during the middle age time frame. The prospering material industry of old and archaic India, especially the development of fine cotton and silk textures, turned out to be around the world prestigious. These materials were sought after across the Bedouin Landmass, Southeast Asia, and even Europe. The Indian subcontinent's cotton and silk exchange assumed a significant part laying out India as a worldwide center point for materials.

The Mughal Realm, which administered India from the mid sixteenth to the mid-eighteenth 100 years, kept on encouraging monetary and modern development. The Mughals advanced assembling, exchange, and artworks, and subject to their authority, India was known for creating great products like multifaceted materials, adornments, and metalwork. The period saw the advancement of shipping lanes and metropolitan focuses, further adding to the development of India's modern scene.

The appearance of the English East India Organization in the seventeenth century significantly affected India's modern process. The English tried to take advantage of India's tremendous assets, and after some time, the Indian economy was rebuilt to serve English interests. India's material industry, which had once been a worldwide pioneer, confronted the presentation of English fabricated materials and exchange limitations that sabotaged its seriousness.

The English pilgrim period saw the foundation of different enterprises in India, basically to serve the interests of the provincial organization. Ventures like materials, steel, and shipbuilding were grown, yet they frequently worked under English control. Indian business and industrialization were smothered as the English zeroed in on extricating assets from India as opposed to cultivating its financial autonomy.

In spite of the difficult frontier climate, a few Indian business visionaries and industrialists arose during this period. Conspicuous figures like Jamsetji Goodbye, a trailblazer of the Indian steel industry, and Ardeshir Godrej, who established the Godrej Gathering, made huge commitments to India's modern scene. These visionaries challenged the chances and established the groundwork for Indian modern development.

The mid twentieth century denoted a time of tremendous change in India's modern process. The opportunity battle contrary to English pilgrim rule concurred with endeavors to advance industrialization and financial independence. Pioneers like Mahatma Gandhi and Jawaharlal Nehru perceived the significance of modern advancement in accomplishing confidence.

The Mahatma pushed for cabin enterprises, advancing hand-turned and hand-woven materials for of monetary strengthening for provincial networks. This development, known as the Swadeshi Development, expected to blacklist English merchandise as well as stressed the meaning of privately delivered and hand tailored items.

Jawaharlal Nehru, India's most memorable Top state leader subsequent to acquiring freedom, was serious areas of strength for a for industrialization. He started a progression of five-year designs that expected to lay out serious areas of strength for a base in India. These plans zeroed in on key areas like steel, energy, and large equipment. The foundation of public area undertakings like Steel Authority of India Restricted (SAIL) and Bharat Weighty Electricals Restricted (BHEL) stamped huge achievements in India's modern process.

The period following India's freedom in 1947 saw the fast development of a few modern areas. The Green Transformation during the 1960s achieved critical expansions in horticultural efficiency, changing India from a food-shortage country to one with excess grain creation. The horticultural and modern areas turned out to be firmly entwined, as modern development worked with the motorization of farming, prompting expanded food creation and worked on provincial vocations.

The development of weighty enterprises in India, especially in areas like steel, concrete, and energy, established the groundwork for the country's modern strength. The foundation of public area endeavors assumed a basic part in fostering the framework and assembling capacities fundamental for financial turn of events. These businesses made positions, invigorate financial development, and upgrade the country's independence.

The car area arose as a vital participant in India's modern scene during the last 50% of the twentieth 100 years. Organizations like Goodbye Engines, Mahindra and Mahindra, and Bajaj Auto became pioneers in the development of vehicles, going from business trucks to bikes. The car business gave work valuable open doors, invigorated advancement, and contributed fundamentally to the country's monetary development.

The product and data innovation (IT) industry became perhaps of the most groundbreaking area in India's modern process. Starting during the 1980s and 1990s, the IT area quickly extended, driven by India's accomplished and English-talking labor force. Organizations like Goodbye Consultancy Administrations (TCS), Infosys, and Wipro became worldwide forerunners in IT administrations and programming improvement. India's IT industry added to financial development as well as assumed a basic part in India's rise as a worldwide innovation center.

India's drug industry additionally saw astounding development. Organizations like Dr. Reddy's Labs and Sun Drugs became noticeable players in the worldwide drug market. The business' development was driven by India's aptitude in synthetic union, innovative work abilities, and practical creation processes.

India's commitments to the worldwide drug market were especially obvious during the HIV/Helps emergency. Indian drug organizations, through the creation of reasonable conventional antiretroviral drugs, assumed an essential part in extending admittance to treatment for a large number of individuals in non-industrial nations.

The 21st century achieved further change in India's modern scene. The ascent of the web based business industry, drove by organizations like Flipkart and Amazon India, upset the retail area. These stages gave potential open doors to private companies and business visionaries to arrive at a more extensive client base.

Sustainable power and clean innovation enterprises have likewise acquired noticeable quality in India. The country's obligation to tending to ecological difficulties and lessening its carbon impression has prompted critical interests in sun powered and wind energy. India has turned into a forerunner in environmentally friendly power creation and has gained significant headway in lessening its reliance on petroleum products.

India's space program, with the Indian Space Exploration Association (ISRO) at its steerage, has taken wonderful steps. ISRO's accomplishments, including effective missions to the Moon and Mars, have exhibited India's capacities in space investigation and satellite innovation.

The space area has not just added to India's logical and innovative headways however has additionally prompted business amazing open doors, like sending off satellites for different nations.

The development of India's modern scene is firmly connected to the country's enterprising soul. India's various new companies and little and medium-sized ventures (SMEs) play had a crucial impact in cultivating development and monetary development. Business visionaries across different areas, from innovation and online business to biotechnology and sustainable power, have been main thrusts behind India's modern advancement.

Government strategies have likewise assumed a critical part in molding India's modern process. Drives, for example, "Make in India," which expects to advance homegrown assembling, have looked to support interests in enterprises like hardware, safeguard, and drugs. The "Advanced India" crusade has zeroed in on improving computerized framework and network, setting out open doors for the tech business and advanced business.

The "Startup India" program has offered help and motivators for new undertakings, encouraging advancement and business venture. Also, financial changes and advancement measures during the 1990s, frequently alluded to as "monetary progression" or "LPG" (Advancement, Privatization, and Globalization), opened India to worldwide business sectors, empowering unfamiliar ventures and exchange.

Notwithstanding, India's modern process has likewise confronted difficulties. Framework impediments, regulatory administrative noise, and work issues have on occasion ruined the country's advancement.

The differences in modern improvement among metropolitan and rustic regions, as well as among various states, stay a worry. Tending to these difficulties is critical for accomplishing a more evenhanded and manageable modern scene.

The accounts of India's modern process are about monetary development and innovative headway as well as about the large numbers of people who have been important for this groundbreaking system. Business people, workers, researchers, engineers, and innumerable others have added to forming India's modern scene. Their endeavors have animated monetary development as well as prompted upgrades in training, wellbeing.

5.3 The challenges and opportunities faced by the workforce.

The labor force of any country is its spine, and its wellbeing and flexibility are critical for financial development and cultural advancement. In the 21st hundred years, the worldwide labor force faces a bunch of difficulties and valuable open doors that have been formed by mechanical headways, moving socioeconomics, monetary changes, and developing workplaces. This conversation investigates the complex scene that the contemporary labor force explores, from the deterrents that should be addressed to the possibilities for development and improvement.

Perhaps of the most noticeable test confronting the labor force in the 21st century is the fast speed of mechanical progression. Mechanization, man-made reasoning (computer based intelligence), and advanced mechanics have changed businesses and occupation markets, prompting worries about work removal and expertise outdated nature. Laborers across different areas are defied with the need to adjust to an innovation driven workplace.

Computerization, which is especially apparent in assembling, coordinated factors, and authoritative undertakings, can possibly further develop efficiency and proficiency. Notwithstanding, it likewise presents a test to laborers whose jobs might become robotized, prompting worries about joblessness and pay imbalance. The effect of computerization reaches out past common laborers, influencing middle class callings too.

As machines become more modern and equipped for performing complex errands, laborers need to foster an alternate arrangement of abilities to stay important in the gig market. Computerization has prompted a developing interest for laborers with mastery in programming, information examination, and computerized education. People who can use innovation to upgrade their efficiency are bound to flourish in the developing labor force.

Artificial intelligence and AI are likewise changing businesses like medical care, money, and client support. These advances can possibly further develop dynamic cycles, offer customized types of assistance, and smooth out activities. In any case, they bring up moral issues in regards to information security, algorithmic predisposition, and the likely loss of occupations to simulated intelligence frameworks.

In the midst of these difficulties, the labor force has potential chances to use innovation for individual and expert development. Web based learning stages and advanced assets empower laborers to gain new abilities and information. The gig economy, which has extended lately, offers adaptable work courses of action that can be invaluable to those looking for assorted revenue sources and independence.

One more huge test looked by the labor force is the effect of the Coronavirus pandemic. The pandemic sped up patterns in remote work and advanced change, reshaping the elements of the working environment. Many organizations needed to rapidly adjust to remote workplaces to guarantee business congruity and worker security. This shift brought the two difficulties and open doors.

Remote work introduced difficulties connected with availability, online protection, and keeping up with balance between fun and serious activities. Laborers confronted detachment, obscured limits among individual and expert life, and expanded screen time. The pandemic additionally featured differences in admittance to remote work open doors, for certain callings and enterprises being more versatile than others.

Notwithstanding, remote work likewise presented new open doors for work-life adaptability and a diminished requirement for driving.

Numerous representatives found they could be comparably useful, while possibly not all the more in this way, while telecommuting. Organizations understood that they could take advantage of a worldwide ability pool and lessen office space costs. Thus, remote and cross breed work plans are probably going to stay an element of the post-pandemic labor force.

The pandemic additionally highlighted the significance of psychological well-being and prosperity in the work environment. Numerous laborers confronted expanded pressure and uneasiness because of the vulnerability and interruption brought about by the pandemic. Organizations started to focus on representative prosperity, offering psychological well-being assets and backing administrations.

The pandemic additionally caused to notice the medical care and fundamental laborers who were on the bleeding edges, gambling with their wellbeing to offer basic types of assistance. These specialists confronted difficulties connected with wellbeing, burnout, and profound trouble. Notwithstanding, their devotion and versatility were perceived and celebrated by networks around the world, featuring the significance of esteeming and supporting fundamental laborers.

Segment changes are one more part of the labor force scene that presents the two difficulties and open doors. In numerous nations, populaces are maturing, prompting a contracting workforce and expanded interest for medical services and senior consideration administrations. A maturing labor force brings insight and mastery yet additionally suggests conversation starters about progression arranging and information move.

The rising variety of the labor force is another segment shift. Associations are perceiving the worth of variety and consideration in driving development and seriousness. In any case, cultivating a comprehensive work environment stays a test, as it requires tending to predisposition and segregation while advancing fairness and value.

Orientation uniformity is a huge issue in the labor force. Ladies have made progress in separating boundaries in generally male-overwhelmed fields, however orientation pay holes and underrepresentation in positions of authority continue. The #MeToo development has brought issues of inappropriate behavior and orientation segregation to the front, inciting conversations and strategy changes.

Amazing open doors for tending to these difficulties incorporate carrying out variety and consideration drives, advancing mentorship and sponsorship programs, and instituting approaches that help balance between fun and serious activities and parental leave. Orientation correspondence isn't just a question of equity and decency yet additionally can possibly support efficiency and monetary development.

The ascent of the gig economy and independent work is reshaping the business scene. These forward thinking work game plans extend to adaptability yet in addition bring vulnerabilities connected with employment opportunity security, advantages, and pay soundness. Laborers in the gig economy frequently miss the mark on customary securities and advantages of regular work, for example, medical coverage, retirement designs, and paid leave.

Also, the gig economy brings up issues about the characterization of laborers as self employed entities or representatives. Legitimate and administrative systems need to adjust to guarantee that gig laborers approach social wellbeing nets and work securities. In certain nations, there are continuous discussions about laborer characterization and freedoms.

The independent and gig economy likewise offer open doors for people to differentiate their revenue sources, investigate innovative undertakings, and accomplish more prominent balance between fun and serious activities. Computerized stages and commercial centers have made it more straightforward for consultants to interface with clients and access a worldwide market.

In the 21st 100 years, the labor force is progressively formed by the quest for maintainability and corporate social obligation. Organizations and workers are perceiving the significance of earth capable practices and moral navigation. Maintainability drives are setting out open doors for green positions, especially in sustainable power, eco-accommodating assembling, and protection endeavors.

The manageability development isn't just a moral objective yet in addition an upper hand for organizations. Customers are progressively looking for items and administrations that line up with their qualities, and organizations that take on supportable practices are probably going to acquire an upper hand. Manageability additionally impacts supply chains, with an accentuation on diminishing waste and limiting ecological effect.

The labor force additionally faces difficulties connected with abilities holes and instructive differences. In a time of quickly developing innovation and information, the interest for explicit abilities frequently dominates the accessibility of laborers with those abilities. This abilities hole can prevent financial development and advancement.

Tending to abilities holes requires a purposeful exertion from instructive establishments, organizations, and legislatures to give preparing and reskilling open doors. Deep rooted learning has become fundamental for laborers to stay versatile and serious in the gig market. Online courses, professional preparation, and apprenticeships offer open doors for upskilling and reskilling.

Labor force instruction and improvement are not restricted to customary scholarly establishments. Organizations are putting resources into worker preparing and improvement projects to outfit their labor force with the vital abilities. Nonstop learning and expert improvement have become necessary parts of profession movement.

The difficulties and valuable open doors confronting the labor force are likewise connected to the more extensive worldwide economy. Financial globalization has brought interconnectedness, permitting organizations and laborers to get to worldwide business sectors and team up across borders. This globalization presents amazing open doors for exchange, venture, and the trading of information.

Notwithstanding, monetary globalization additionally presents difficulties, like financial unpredictability, exchange uneven characters, and pay imbalance. Laborers in created nations might confront contest from lower-wage work markets, while agricultural nations might battle to get to worldwide business sectors based on equivalent conditions. These incongruities call for fair exchange approaches and endeavors to address worldwide financial disparities.

The labor force of the 21st century is additionally exploring the intricacies of information security and online protection. As the advanced economy grows, people and associations should shield delicate data from digital dangers and information breaks. The approach of remote work and the digitalization of administrations has intensified the significance of strong network protection measures.

Information security concerns have incited guidelines, like the European Association's Overall Information Assurance Guideline (GDPR) and the California Customer Protection Act (CCPA), which put more prominent accentuation on people's control.

6 |

Chapter 6

"The Promise of Technology"

The development of innovation has been a characterizing part of human advancement since forever ago, from the earliest creations like the haggle furrow to the cutting edge wonders of computerized reasoning and quantum registering. Innovation has generally modified the manner in which we live, work, impart, and take care of issues. In the 21st hundred years, innovation holds the commitment of considerably more prominent progressions, with the possibility to address squeezing worldwide difficulties and work on the personal satisfaction for individuals all over the planet.

The underpinning of current innovation lies in the logical revelations and developments of the past. The nineteenth and twentieth hundreds of years saw momentous advancements in physical science, science, and designing, which laid the foundation for the data age. The development of the message, phone, and radio reformed significant distance correspondence, empowering the trading of data and thoughts across the globe.

The rise of the PC denoted an essential crossroads in mankind's set of experiences. Early PCs were huge, room-filling machines with restricted handling power. In any case, they set up for the computerized transformation by presenting the idea of paired code, consistent tasks, and information stockpiling. The quick progression of processing innovation, driven by pioneers like Alan Turing and John von Neumann, prompted the making of more modest, all the more impressive, and more adaptable PCs.

In 1947, the advancement of the semiconductor at Ringer Labs reformed hardware. Semiconductors supplanted vacuum tubes, making gadgets more modest, more effective, and less inclined to overheating. This advanced prepared for the cutting edge central processor, which is at the core of practically all electronic gadgets, from cell phones to satellites.

The creation of the coordinated circuit (IC) in the last part of the 1950s by Jack Kilby and Robert Noyce denoted one more achievement in innovation's direction. The IC permitted various electronic parts to be scaled down and put on a solitary chip, definitely lessening the size and cost of electronic gadgets. This development prompted the expansion of purchaser gadgets, from number crunchers and PCs to cell phones and shrewd apparatuses.

The ascent of the web in the late twentieth century addressed an extraordinary second in innovation and correspondence. Initially created as an examination organization, the Internet, made by Tim Berners-Lee, empowered the consistent sharing of data across the globe. The web associated individuals, organizations, and legislatures, upsetting the manner in which we access and trade information, lead business, and speak with each other.

The multiplication of cell phones, combined with propels in remote correspondence innovation, carried the web under the control of billions of individuals. Cell phones, with their processing power, web availability, and a variety of uses, have become omnipresent apparatuses for correspondence, efficiency, amusement, and data access. The blend of versatility and availability has brought about the time of the "consistently on" society.

The commitment of innovation is maybe most strikingly exemplified in the domain of medical services. Clinical innovation has taken unbelievable steps in working on quiet consideration, diagnostics, and treatment. The advancement of clinical imaging innovations, for example, X-beams, attractive reverberation imaging (X-ray), and registered tomography (CT) examines, has empowered specialists to determine infections and conditions to have extraordinary exactness. These advancements have become fundamental in persistent consideration and have added to expanded future and worked on personal satisfaction.

The area of biotechnology has prompted the improvement of imaginative medicines and treatments. Hereditary designing and quality altering advances, like CRISPR-Cas9, have opened new roads for treating hereditary sicknesses and problems. The commitment of customized medication, custom-made to a singular's exceptional hereditary cosmetics, holds the possibility to reform medical services by advancing therapy designs and limiting unfavorable impacts.

Telemedicine, worked with by advanced innovation, has acquired noticeable quality, particularly during the Coronavirus pandemic. It empowers patients to talk with medical care suppliers from a distance, extending admittance to clinical benefits and decreasing the requirement for in-person visits. Telemedicine can possibly further develop medical services conveyance, especially in underserved and distant regions.

Man-made consciousness (artificial intelligence) and AI are driving development in medical services, helping with sickness determination, drug revelation, and therapy arranging. Computer based intelligence calculations can break down clinical pictures, recognize oddities, and foresee patient results, adding to additional exact and opportune clinical intercessions.

AI models are being utilized to recognize potential medication up-and-comers and speed up drug improvement.

The combination of wearable gadgets and wellbeing observing applications has enabled people to assume responsibility for their wellbeing. Gadgets like smartwatches can follow imperative signs, screen actual work, and give early admonitions of potential medical problems. These devices advance preventive medical services and energize a better way of life.

The commitment of innovation stretches out to tending to worldwide difficulties, especially with regards to maintainable turn of events. Natural worries, for example, environmental change and asset consumption, have provoked the improvement of clean advancements and sustainable power arrangements. Sunlight based chargers, wind turbines, and energy-effective advances have taken huge steps in lessening ozone depleting substance outflows and relieving the effect of environmental change.

The Web of Things (IoT) is an innovative idea that interfaces regular items to the web, permitting them to gather and trade information. IoT has applications in farming, transportation, energy the board, and medical care. For instance, in agribusiness, IoT sensors can screen soil conditions and harvest wellbeing, enhancing asset use and expanding crop yields.

Perfect and environmentally friendly power innovations, including sun based and wind power, have progressed fundamentally, adding to a change away from non-renewable energy sources. Electric vehicles, controlled by feasible energy sources, have become progressively well known, diminishing ozone depleting substance outflows in the transportation area. Developments in energy capacity, like lithium-particle batteries, are vital for upgrading the dependability of environmentally friendly power sources.

In metropolitan preparation and transportation, innovation vows to address difficulties connected with gridlock, contamination, and energy proficiency. Brilliant urban communities are utilizing information examination, sensors, and correspondence organizations to advance transportation frameworks, oversee assets, and upgrade the personal satisfaction for inhabitants. Independent vehicles and wise traffic the board frameworks can possibly lessen mishaps and further develop traffic stream.

The field of room investigation is seeing noteworthy mechanical headways, with the commitment of extending how we might interpret the universe and possibly giving answers for natural difficulties. Space organizations and privately owned businesses are creating progressed impetus frameworks, rocket, and investigation apparatuses. The fruitful sending of room telescopes, similar to the Hubble Space Telescope and the James Webb Space Telescope, has developed our insight into the universe.

Space-based innovations have applications past cosmology and astronomy. Earth perception satellites assume a critical part in observing the climate, following weather conditions, and evaluating the effects of cataclysmic events. Satellites furnished with remote detecting instruments give important information to farming, ranger service, calamity the board, and metropolitan preparation.

The commitment of innovation reaches out to working on instructive open doors and availability. Web based learning stages and advanced assets have democratized schooling, empowering individuals to get to information and get new abilities from basically anyplace. Gigantic open web-based courses (MOOCs) and e-learning stages offer many courses and degrees, taking care of different instructive requirements and interests.

Man-made brainpower is likewise being utilized in schooling to customize opportunities for growth, distinguish regions where understudies might require extra help, and improve the adequacy of educating materials. Instructive organizations and ed-tech organizations are utilizing man-made intelligence calculations to adjust content to individual learning styles, guaranteeing that understudies get custom fitted guidance.

The utilization of computer generated reality (VR) and expanded reality (AR) in schooling can possibly reform growth opportunities. VR can move understudies to verifiable occasions or far off areas, making learning seriously captivating and vivid. AR can overlay computerized data onto the actual world, improving the comprehension of complicated ideas in different subjects.

The openness of data and the capacity to team up across geological limits have changed exploration and advancement. Logical headways frequently depend on worldwide joint effort, with analysts from various nations cooperating to address complex difficulties. Admittance to immense information bases, research papers, and online assets has sped up the speed of disclosure and development.

The democratization of data and innovation can possibly engage people and networks. Online stages and web-based entertainment have intensified voices, empowered activism, and achieved social and political change. Publicly supporting and crowdfunding stages have given open doors to people to raise reserves, assemble backing, and transform inventive thoughts into the real world.

Innovation has likewise assumed a critical part in misfortune reaction and recuperation endeavors. Correspondence innovations, including web-based entertainment, have worked with quick reaction and coordination during cataclysmic events and emergencies. Drones and remotely worked vehicle.

6.1 The role of technology and innovation in the steel industry.

The steel business has for some time been a foundation of current economies, giving the fundamental material to framework, development, transportation, and endless different ventures. Steel is a flexible and solid material, yet its creation has gone through huge change throughout the long term, to a great extent because of the job of innovation and development. In this conversation, we will investigate the fundamental job that innovation and development play in the steel business, from the beginning of steelmaking to the present and what's in store.

Authentic Development of Steelmaking

The historical backdrop of steel traces all the way back to old times when it was basically delivered through work escalated strategies like bloomery refining, which included warming iron metal in a heater with charcoal. These early strategies were restricted as far as both the amount and nature of steel delivered. It was only after the improvement of the Bessemer cycle in the nineteenth century that steel creation saw a critical mechanical jump.

The Bessemer cycle, designed by Sir Henry Bessemer in 1856, upset steelmaking by acquainting a technique with convert liquid iron into steel by blowing air through it to eliminate contaminations. This advancement emphatically expanded the creation of steel and worked on its quality, making steel more reasonable and available. The Bessemer cycle was a vital crossroads throughout the entire existence of the steel business, denoting the start of large scale manufacturing and driving industrialization.

Ensuing developments, like the open-hearth process and the fundamental oxygen heater (BOF), further refined steelmaking techniques. The advancement of these cycles worked on the nature of steel and extended its scope of utilizations. Steel turned into a fundamental material for foundation, including scaffolds, rail routes, and structures.

The Job of Innovation in Current Steelmaking

The steel business has kept on developing, with innovation and development assuming a focal part in each part of creation, from unrefined components to the end result. A portion of the critical mechanical headways in present day steelmaking include:

Unrefined substance Refinement: The nature of steel begins with the unrefined components. Developments in mining and metal handling have worked on the proficiency of iron mineral extraction and filtration. Mechanization, remote detecting, and advanced mechanics have been utilized to make mining tasks more secure and more productive.

Electric Circular segment Heaters (EAF): The electric bend heater is a urgent innovation in steelmaking. It utilizes power to liquefy scrap steel and produce new steel. EAF innovation is especially significant for reusing and maintainability endeavors as it takes into consideration the utilization of scrap steel as an unrefined substance. This interaction is more energy-effective and harmless to the ecosystem contrasted with customary impact heaters.

Constant Projecting: Ceaseless projecting is a technique that produces steel in a consistent, strong structure as opposed to conventional ingots. This cycle lessens squander, upgrades item quality, and further develops effectiveness underway.

Alloying and Concentrated Prepares: The advancement of particular prepares, including high-strength, erosion safe, and intensity safe compounds, has extended the scope of steel applications. These specific prepares are utilized in aviation, car, development, and different enterprises.

Mechanization and Mechanical technology: The steel business has taken on robotization and advanced mechanics in different creation processes. Mechanized frameworks have further developed security, accuracy, and productivity in steel fabricating. Robots are many times utilized in undertakings that are perilous or require high accuracy.

Digitalization and Industry 4.0: The steel business is embracing Industry 4.0 standards, which include the joining of advanced innovations and the web of things (IoT) into assembling processes. This empowers constant checking, prescient support, and information driven navigation.

Supportability Drives: Maintainability has turned into a basic concentration in the steel business. Developments in energy proficiency, carbon catch, and reusing have prompted all the more harmless to the ecosystem steel creation strategies. Steelmakers are effectively attempting to diminish their carbon impression and improve their manageability rehearses.

Difficulties and Valuable open doors in the Steel Business

The steel business faces the two difficulties and open doors in the 21st hundred years, and innovation assumes a focal part in tending to them:

Natural Worries: One of the most squeezing difficulties for the steel business is lessening its ecological effect. Customary steel creation techniques are energy-serious and bring about significant fossil fuel by-products. Imaginative advances, for example, hydrogen-based steelmaking and carbon catch and usage, hold the possibility to make steel creation more supportable and diminish its carbon impression.

Reusing and Round Economy: Steel is a profoundly recyclable material, and the business has a valuable chance to lead in the improvement of a roundabout economy. The utilization of electric curve heaters and reusing processes lessens the requirement for essential iron mineral and saves assets. Innovation and development can additionally improve the productivity and extent of steel reusing.

Market Requests: Market requests for steel are continually evolving. Mechanical progressions in the auto business, for instance, have prompted expanded interest for cutting edge high-strength prepares. Adjusting to advancing business sector needs and remaining in front of contenders requires constant advancement in steel item improvement.

Worldwide Rivalry: The steel business is profoundly cutthroat on a worldwide scale. Mechanical development is a critical consider keeping up with intensity. Organizations that put resources into innovative work, process enhancement, and maintainability measures are better situated to flourish in a worldwide market.

Advanced Change: The computerized change of the steel business presents the two difficulties and open doors. While taking on computerized innovations can upgrade proficiency and seriousness, it likewise requires critical speculations and a gifted labor force. The business should explore the intricacies of information security and protection.

Labor force Difficulties: As the business turns out to be progressively robotized, there is a requirement for a profoundly talented labor force that can work and keep up with cutting edge hardware. The business should put resources into preparing and schooling to guarantee a labor force that can really use new innovations.

Future Advancements in Steelmaking

The steel business proceeds to develop, and future advancements are supposed to shape the business' direction:

Hydrogen-Based Steelmaking: Quite possibly of the main advancement not too far off is hydrogen-based steelmaking. Hydrogen can possibly supplant carbon in the steel creation process, lessening fossil fuel byproducts. Green hydrogen, delivered utilizing environmentally friendly power sources, is especially encouraging for economical steelmaking.

Carbon Catch and Usage (CCU): CCU advances mean to catch fossil fuel byproducts from steel creation and use them in different applications, like the development of engineered fills or synthetic substances. CCU is a significant part of the business' endeavors to diminish its carbon impression.

Added substance Assembling: 3D printing and added substance fabricating can possibly alter how steel parts are delivered. This innovation considers complex, redid, and more proficient plans, decreasing waste and further developing asset use.

Savvy Manufacturing plants: The steel business is progressively taking on the idea of brilliant production lines, where advanced innovations and information investigation are utilized for continuous checking, prescient upkeep, and interaction enhancement. These advancements upgrade effectiveness, diminish personal time, and further develop item quality.

High level Materials: Examination into cutting edge materials, including graphene and carbon nanotubes, is continuous. These materials can possibly make more grounded, lighter, and more sturdy steel items with many applications, from development to aviation.

Ecological Stewardship: As natural worries become more articulated, steel organizations are putting resources into feasible practices. This incorporates endeavors to limit water utilization, lessen energy utilization, and breaking point squander age.

Coordinated effort and Exploration: Cooperation between steel organizations, research foundations, and states is imperative for driving advancement in the business. Associations can prompt leap forwards in innovation, process streamlining, and supportability.

6.2 The adoption of modern manufacturing techniques.

Producing plays had a focal impact in the development and improvement of economies around the world. From the earliest long stretches of craftsmanship to the modern upheaval, and into the present, how merchandise are delivered has persistently advanced. In ongoing many years, the reception of present day fabricating methods has been a basic driver of development, proficiency, and seriousness across ventures. This conversation digs into the change of assembling and the key elements impacting the boundless reception of present day strategies.

Authentic Advancement of Assembling

Fabricating has gone through significant changes from the beginning of time, with every period portrayed by particular creation strategies. The authentic advancement of assembling can be extensively classified as follows:

Craftsmanship: In pre-modern social orders, fabricating was transcendently described by craftsmanship. Gifted craftsmans created items manually, with restricted apparatuses and assets. While this approach took into consideration unpredictably planned and modified products, the time had come consuming and had restricted versatility.

Modern Unrest: The eighteenth and nineteenth hundreds of years denoted the coming of the modern upset, a time of extremist change in assembling. Automation, controlled by steam motors and later electric engines, empowered the large scale manufacturing of products in processing plants. Sequential construction systems and tradable parts became fundamental parts of this period, exemplified by crafted by figures like Eli Whitney and Henry Passage.

Robotization and Computerization: The mid-twentieth century saw the presentation of mechanization and computerization in assembling. The utilization of mathematical control (NC) and PC mathematical control (CNC) machines considered more noteworthy accuracy and repeatability underway. Robots and programmable rationale regulators (PLCs) assumed a focal part in this robotization cycle.

Current Assembling: The current time is set apart by a shift toward present day producing procedures. These incorporate cutting edge innovations like added substance fabricating (3D printing), the Web of Things (IoT), man-made consciousness (computer based intelligence), and information examination. These advances are driving the reception of shrewd manufacturing plants and Industry 4.0, prompting more noteworthy productivity, adaptability, and customization underway.

Key Variables Driving the Reception of Current Assembling Strategies

A few variables have met to drive the far reaching reception of current assembling procedures lately. These elements are reshaping the assembling scene and impacting organizations to embrace creative innovations and practices.

Worldwide Rivalry: The globalization of business sectors and the ascent of global contest have placed tension on makers to further develop effectiveness and diminish costs. Current assembling strategies empower organizations to stay serious in a worldwide commercial center.

Client Assumptions: The present shoppers have better standards for item quality, customization, and fast conveyance. Present day fabricating procedures consider more noteworthy adaptability in fulfilling these needs, giving customized items and fast reaction times.

Fast Mechanical Headways: The speed increase of innovative progressions, particularly in regions like advanced mechanics, simulated intelligence, and materials science, has made it more useful and practical for makers to take on current methods. 3D printing, for instance, has become more open and reasonable, empowering a large number of enterprises to utilize added substance producing.

Cost Decrease: Present day fabricating procedures can prompt expense decreases in more than one way. Mechanization and mechanical technology can diminish work costs, while prescient upkeep and IoT can lessen personal time and support costs. The reception of energy-effective advancements additionally adds to cost investment funds.

Asset Proficiency: Supportability is a developing concern, and current assembling methods offer open doors for expanded asset productivity. Added substance producing, for instance, creates less waste than conventional subtractive techniques. Also, IoT and information investigation can assist with improving energy and asset utilization.

Store network Flexibility: Late disturbances in worldwide stockpile chains, for example, those brought about by the Coronavirus pandemic, have highlighted the requirement for more noteworthy versatility. Current assembling methods, including computerized twins and high level coordinated operations, can improve inventory network the board, making it more versatile and strong.

Customization and Personalization: Purchaser inclinations are moving toward additional redid and customized items. Current assembling methods, like 3D printing and high level CNC machining, empower organizations to offer fitted answers for their clients.

Key Current Assembling Methods

The reception of current assembling methods incorporates a wide exhibit of innovations and practices. Here are a portion of the key methods that are molding the fate of assembling:

Added substance Assembling (3D Printing): Added substance producing is a pivotal procedure that forms objects layer by layer. It takes into consideration mind boggling plans, fast prototyping, and the development of complex, modified parts. Businesses like aviation, medical care, and auto have embraced 3D printing for its adaptability and plan capacities.

Advanced mechanics and Robotization: Advanced mechanics and mechanization are necessary to current assembling. Robots are utilized for assignments going from gathering and welding to material dealing with and quality control. Mechanization increments proficiency, lessens blunders, and upgrades laborer wellbeing.

Web of Things (IoT): IoT includes the availability of gadgets and sensors, permitting information to be gathered and examined progressively. In assembling, IoT can give experiences into machine execution, energy utilization, and store network operations. Prescient upkeep, empowered by IoT, forestalls breakdowns and enhance support plans.

Computerized reasoning (simulated intelligence) and AI: man-made intelligence and AI are utilized to examine tremendous measures of information and pursue forecasts and choices in view of that information. In assembling, man-made intelligence can be applied to quality control, request determining, and process streamlining.

Computerized Twins: An advanced twin is a virtual portrayal of an actual item or framework. Makers utilize computerized twins to reproduce and enhance creation processes, considering better plan, testing, and support.

High level Materials: The improvement of new materials, like composites and superalloys, has extended the conceivable outcomes in assembling. These materials offer improved strength, toughness, and execution for a great many applications.

Savvy Industrial facilities and Industry 4.0: Shrewd production lines are described by the mix of advanced innovations into assembling processes. This idea, frequently alluded to as Industry 4.0, joins IoT, computer based intelligence, and information investigation to make more proficient, adaptable, and responsive creation conditions.

High level Investigation and Information Representation: The utilization of information examination and perception devices assists makers with acquiring experiences from their information. This can prompt interaction enhancements, quality control, and prescient upkeep.

Cooperative Advanced mechanics (Cobots): Cooperative robots work close by human laborers, improving efficiency and wellbeing. Cobots are intended to be handily modified and adaptable, making them reasonable for various errands.

Production network Digitization: The digitization of supply chains incorporates the utilization of innovations like blockchain for recognizability, RFID for continuous following, and information investigation for advancing coordinated factors.

Provokes and Obstructions to Reception

While the reception of current assembling strategies offers various advantages, it additionally presents difficulties and obstructions that producers should address:

High Introductory Expenses: Executing current assembling procedures frequently requires critical capital venture. This incorporates buying progressed gear, preparing workers, and redesiging existing cycles.

Labor force Abilities: The labor force should adjust to new innovations and practices. This might include retraining representatives and recruiting people with mastery in regions like man-made intelligence, IoT, and information examination.

Information Security: The expanded utilization of advanced innovations and information assortment raises worries about information security and protection. Producers should lay out hearty network safety measures to safeguard delicate data.

Reconciliation Difficulties: Coordinating different advances and frameworks can be intricate. Similarity issues can emerge while endeavoring to join different programming and equipment arrangements.

Administrative Consistence: Assembling enterprises are dependent upon guidelines and norms that might should be refreshed to oblige present day methods. Organizations should guarantee consistence while executing new advancements.

Change The executives: The progress to present day producing strategies might require a huge social shift inside an association. Change the board techniques are crucial for gain representative purchase in and guarantee fruitful reception.

Contextual investigations of Present day Assembling Reception

Avionic business: The aeronautic trade has embraced 3D printing for assembling complex parts with decreased weight and expanded strength. GE Flight, for instance, produces 3D-printed fuel spouts for fly motors, bringing about better eco-friendliness and decreased outflows.

Auto Industry: Car makers are progressively involving mechanical technology and robotization for undertakings like welding, painting, and gathering. Tesla's Gigafactories embody the utilization of present day fabricating procedures to productively deliver electric vehicles.

Drug Industry: The drug business has executed present day methods for drug creation, including nonstop assembling and information investigation. These advancements have further developed creation proficiency and quality control.

6.3 The global relevance of Indian steel products.

The worldwide steel industry is a dynamic and pivotal part of the world's assembling and framework improvement. India has arisen as a huge player in this industry, adding to the worldwide stockpile of steel items. The worldwide importance of Indian steel items can be ascribed to a few elements, including the country's significant creation limit, the nature of its steel items, and its effect on different ventures around the world. In this conversation, we will dig into the diverse worldwide significance of Indian steel items and analyze the key factors that add to India's situation in the worldwide steel market.

India's Steel Industry: An Outline

India has a long history of steel creation, tracing all the way back to old times. Notwithstanding, it was during the post-autonomy time frame that the nation's steel industry saw huge development and modernization. The foundation of the Steel Authority of India Restricted (SAIL) and the quick extension of private steel makers, like Goodbye Steel and Jindal Steel and Power, added to the business' turn of events.

India's steel industry has encountered significant development throughout the course of recent many years. Key measurements feature this development:

Creation Limit: India has reliably extended its steel creation limit. In 2020, India was the second-biggest steel maker on the planet, with a rough steel creation limit of more than 100 million metric tons.

Homegrown Utilization: The development of India's economy and foundation advancement has prompted expanded homegrown utilization of steel items. India's steel utilization is supposed to keep on rising, driven by framework tasks, urbanization, and modern development.

Variety of Steel Items: The Indian steel industry makes an extensive variety of steel items, including level and long items, underlying steel, treated steel, and specialty prepares. This variety permits India to all around the world take care of different ventures.

Quality Guidelines: Indian steel makers have made significant interests in working on the nature of their items. Numerous Indian steel plants stick to worldwide quality principles, adding to the seriousness of their items in the worldwide market.

Key Elements Adding to the Worldwide Pertinence of Indian Steel Items

Creation Limit and Commodity: India's critical creation limit has situated it as a significant exporter of steel items. The nation trades different steel items, including hot-moved curls, cold-moved loops, plates, and lines, to various nations. These products add to India's worldwide importance in the steel market.

Cutthroat Valuing: Indian steel makers are frequently ready to offer serious estimating for their items. Lower work and functional expenses contrasted with a few different nations add to cost-proficient creation, making Indian steel items appealing to worldwide buyers.

Quality Affirmation: Numerous Indian steel makers stick to rigid quality control measures. They keep up with accreditations, like ISO and Agency of Indian Norms (BIS) affirmations, guaranteeing that their items satisfy global quality guidelines. This obligation to quality upgrades the worldwide pertinence of Indian steel items.

Different Item Reach: Indian steel makers produce an extensive variety of steel items to address the issues of different enterprises. This variety, including level and long items, treated steel, and specialty prepares, permits Indian producers to successfully serve worldwide business sectors.

Framework Improvement: India's quickly developing foundation advancement area, including development, transportation, and energy, drives homegrown steel utilization. The requirement for quality steel items in these areas brings about expanded creation and product, upgrading India's worldwide importance.

Auto and Assembling Businesses: The Indian steel industry assumes a vital part in supporting the car and assembling areas worldwide. Top notch steel items are utilized in the development of vehicles, apparatus, and gear, adding to the development of these enterprises around the world.

Oil and Gas Industry: India's steel makers give steel items to the oil and gas industry, including pipelines, drill pipes, and different parts. These items are utilized worldwide in the investigation, creation, and transportation of oil and gas assets.

Tempered Steel and Unique Composites: India is a remarkable maker of treated steel and extraordinary compounds, which are utilized in businesses like synthetics, petrochemicals, drugs, and food handling. The worldwide interest for hardened steel and exceptional composites further highlights India's worldwide significance.

Span Development: The creation of underlying steel assumes a huge part in span development projects all over the planet. India's steel makers add to worldwide foundation advancement by providing primary steel for spans and other basic framework.

Worldwide Effect of Indian Steel Items

Indian steel items altogether affect different ventures around the world. A few striking regions where Indian steel items are significant include:

Development Industry: Indian steel items, including primary steel, are utilized in development projects around the world. They add to the advancement of structures, spans, and other framework, supporting development enterprises around the world.

Car Industry: The car business depends on Indian steel items for assembling vehicles and parts. Indian steel is utilized in the creation of vehicles, trucks, and different vehicles, influencing the auto area on a worldwide scale.

Energy Area: Steel items from India are fundamental in the energy area, including oil and gas. They are utilized in the development of pipelines, penetrating gear, and parts for energy extraction and transportation.

Assembling and Hardware: The assembling and apparatus ventures rely upon Indian steel items for the creation of apparatus, gear, and assembling devices utilized across different areas worldwide.

Framework and Development: Indian steel items add to the worldwide advancement of foundation, including interstates, rail routes, air terminals, and extensions. They are utilized in the development of basic framework projects around the world.

Oil and Gas Investigation: Steel items from India are utilized in the investigation and extraction of oil and gas assets, supporting the worldwide energy industry.

Synthetic and Petrochemical Ventures: Treated steel and extraordinary combinations from India are essential in the substance, petrochemical, drug, and food handling businesses. These materials are utilized in hardware and offices around the world.

Difficulties and Future Open doors

While Indian steel items have taken critical steps in the worldwide market, they likewise face difficulties and future open doors:

Challenges:

Contest: The worldwide steel industry is profoundly cutthroat, with various nations competing for piece of the pie. India faces rivalry from nations like China, the US, and Japan.

Natural Guidelines: Severe ecological guidelines and manageability worries in the development of steel might present difficulties. Sticking to supportable and eco-accommodating practices is urgent for keeping up with worldwide significance.

Mechanical Progressions: Keeping up to date with innovative headways, for example, Industry 4.0 and robotization, is fundamental for keeping up with proficiency and quality in steel creation.

Exchange Obstructions: Exchange hindrances and protectionist estimates in different nations can influence the commodity of Indian steel items.

Future Open doors:

Manageable Works on: Embracing economical works on, including energy-effective and low-discharge advances, can situate Indian steel items as harmless to the ecosystem choices in the worldwide market.

Innovative work: Proceeded with interests in innovative work can prompt the improvement of cutting edge steel items with exceptional properties and applications.

Esteem Option: Zeroing in on esteem added steel items, for example, high-strength prepares and high level materials, can set out new open doors in enterprises like aviation and car.

Coordinated effort: Coordinated efforts with worldwide accomplices, research organizations, and industry affiliations can prompt advancement and the improvement of universally serious steel items.

7 |

Chapter 7

"Global Partnerships and Trade"

The elements of worldwide associations and exchange have gone through critical changes throughout recent many years. These progressions have been driven by different variables, including mechanical headways, changes in international power, and developing buyer inclinations. In this paper, we will investigate the complexities of worldwide organizations and exchange, diving into the authentic setting, contemporary difficulties, and possible future headings.

Verifiable Setting:

The idea of exchange and organizations on a worldwide scale is essentially as old as human progress itself. From the Silk Street that associated Asia and Europe in antiquated times to the European frontier domains of the sixteenth to nineteenth hundreds of years, exchange and collaboration among various areas and countries have formed the course of history. These verifiable shipping lanes and partnerships were much of the time affected by the quest for important assets, mechanical information, and social trade.

One vital improvement in worldwide exchange was the development of private enterprise and the Modern Upset during the eighteenth and nineteenth hundreds of years. These changes prompted the ascent of a worldwide financial framework where products, capital, and work were progressively interconnected. European powers laid out exchanging settlements across the world, prompting the trading of products like flavors, materials, and valuable metals.

As countries extended their realms and laid out provinces, the financial interdependencies between locales developed. The appearance of the message and steamships in the nineteenth century further sped up worldwide correspondence and transportation, making significant distance exchange more productive. Notwithstanding, this period was likewise set apart by double-dealing and inconsistent exchange connections, with frontier controls frequently benefiting to the detriment of their provinces.

The mid-twentieth century achieved a huge change in the worldwide exchange scene. Following the destruction of The Second Great War, nations tried to make a more steady worldwide request. The Bretton Woods Gathering in 1944 prompted the foundation of organizations like the Global Financial Asset (IMF) and the World Bank, intended to advance monetary participation and improvement. Furthermore, the Overall Settlement on Levies and Exchange (GATT) was made to decrease exchange obstructions, at last advancing into the World Exchange Association (WTO).

During this time, numerous nations acquired freedom from pilgrim rule, trying to partake in the worldwide exchanging framework based on their conditions. This decolonization cycle prompted the enhancement of worldwide exchange accomplices and the rise of new monetary powers, especially in Asia. Prominently, the development of the European Financial People group (EEC) in 1957 denoted a huge move toward local monetary coordination, cultivating collaboration among European countries.

Contemporary Difficulties:

Today, worldwide organizations and exchange face a plenty of perplexing difficulties. One of the most major problems is the pressure between streamlined commerce and protectionism. While globalization has brought financial development and diminished destitution for some, it has likewise prompted pay disparity and occupation relocation in specific districts. This has powered an ascent in protectionist strategies, exemplified in terms of professional career questions between significant economies like the US and China.

Another huge test is environmental change and ecological supportability. As the world turns out to be more interconnected through exchange, the ecological effect of creation and transportation of merchandise has turned into a developing concern. Calls for all the more harmless to the ecosystem exchange rehearses, like lessening fossil fuel byproducts and advancing practical inventory chains, have picked up speed.

The advanced unrest has changed worldwide exchange by empowering web based business and computerized administrations. While this has opened up new open doors, it has likewise raised issues connected with information security, network protection, and licensed innovation privileges. The multiplication of innovation and the web have obscured conventional limits, settling on it fundamental for peaceful accords to address these worries.

Besides, the Coronavirus pandemic featured the delicacy of worldwide inventory chains. The interruption brought about by the pandemic highlighted the requirement for stronger and differentiated production network organizations, with numerous nations rethinking their overreliance on a solitary hotspot for basic merchandise. This has prompted conversations on reshoring and nearshoring, where creation is carried nearer to the buyer market.

International pressures are another key element molding worldwide associations and exchange. The competition between the US and China has critical ramifications for the worldwide financial scene. Exchange debates, taxes, and limitations on innovation moves have brought up issues about the degree to which public safety concerns can be utilized as supports for protectionist measures.

The issue of work freedoms and working circumstances in the worldwide store network is likewise a central issue. Numerous worldwide organizations source their items from agricultural nations with lower work costs, here and there prompting unfortunate working circumstances and abuse. Endeavors to address these worries incorporate global work guidelines and corporate social obligation drives.

Future Bearings:

To explore the difficulties of worldwide associations and exchange, countries and global associations should think about a few future headings. One methodology is to advance more comprehensive and manageable exchange rehearses. This includes guaranteeing that the advantages of exchange are impartially conveyed and that natural and social principles are maintained. Multilateral arrangements, like the Unified Countries Practical Improvement Objectives, can act as a system for advancing these targets.

One more bearing is the enhancement of supply chains and a reestablished center around versatility. The Coronavirus pandemic uncovered weaknesses in worldwide stock chains, provoking nations and organizations to rethink their dependence on a solitary source or locale for basic products. A more expanded approach can upgrade store network strength, diminish dangers, and better plan for future disturbances.

As far as innovation and computerized exchange, global collaboration is critical. As innovation keeps on propelling, nations should cooperate to lay out normal guidelines for information security, network safety, and protected innovation insurance. This can advance trust and empower the free progression of information while defending individual privileges.

International strains request a nuanced and adjusted approach. While contest between significant powers is unavoidable, finding areas of participation and normal interest is fundamental. Global foundations, similar to the Unified Countries and the World Exchange Association, can assume a part in working with discourse and question goal.

Besides, the worldwide local area ought to keep on tending to work freedoms and working circumstances in the production network. Global organizations have an obligation to guarantee that their providers stick to moral work rehearses. States can likewise implement and fortify work norms, and shoppers can assume a part by requesting morally obtained items.

Environmental change presents quite possibly of the most dire test. A change to a more manageable and harmless to the ecosystem worldwide exchange framework is basic. This can be accomplished through measures like carbon estimating, advancing environmentally friendly power sources, and boosting economical practices underway and transportation.

7.1 The international dynamics of India's steel trade.

The steel business holds an essential spot in India's economy, and its worldwide exchange elements have developed fundamentally throughout the long term. As one of the world's biggest makers of steel, India's job in the worldwide steel exchange has become progressively noticeable. In this exposition, we will investigate the global elements of India's steel exchange, looking at its verifiable setting, current status, difficulties, and future possibilities.

Authentic Setting:

India's steel industry has a rich history that can be followed back to old times. Customary techniques for steel creation, for example, the pot steel process, were created in the Indian subcontinent hundreds of years prior. In any case, the advanced steel industry in India started to come to fruition during English frontier rule in the nineteenth hundred years. The provincial organization laid out the Goodbye Iron and Steel Organization (presently Goodbye Steel) in 1907, denoting a huge achievement in India's steel creation.

The post-autonomy period during the twentieth century saw the foundation of a few public area steel plants as a component of the public authority's industrialization endeavors. These plants, under elements like Steel Authority of India Restricted (SAIL) and Rashtriya

Ispat Nigam Restricted (RINL), assumed a vital part in building the groundwork of India's steel industry. During this period, India principally centered around satisfying its homegrown steel need and was a generally minor player in global steel exchange.

In the late twentieth hundred years, financial progression and globalization introduced another period for India's steel industry. The public authority started to destroy the permit raj framework and open up the economy. This approach shift energized private area interests in steel creation, prompting the development of a few confidential steel organizations, like Jindal Steel and Power, Essar Steel, and JSW Steel. Accordingly, India's steel creation limit extended fundamentally, and the nation began making its presence felt on the worldwide stage.

Current Status:

Today, India remains as one of the world's biggest steel makers, with a yearly creation limit of north of 100 million metric tons. This development in limit has been driven by interests in present day steel plants and mechanical headways.

Indian steel organizations have embraced cutting edge strategies and cycles to further develop creation productivity and quality, making them serious in the worldwide market.

The worldwide elements of India's steel exchange are portrayed by the two commodities and imports. India trades an assortment of steel items to various nations, including semi-endlessly completed steel items like hot-moved curls, cold-moved loops, and steel pipes. Significant commodity objections for Indian steel incorporate the US, the Unified Bedouin Emirates, Vietnam, and a few other Asian and Center Eastern nations. India's upper hand in the worldwide steel market is its capacity to deliver steel at a lower cost because of elements like less expensive work and unrefined components.

On the import side, India additionally gets critical amounts of steel, basically as high-grade steel, unique steel, and certain worth added steel items. These imports take care of explicit modern and framework needs inside the country. In any case, this has prompted worries about exchange uneven characters and the need to find some kind of harmony among imports and homegrown creation.

Challenges:

While India's steel industry has gained striking headway, it faces a few difficulties in its global exchange elements. One of the critical difficulties is the unpredictability of worldwide steel costs. Steel costs are impacted by a perplexing interaction of elements, including unrefined substance costs, worldwide interest, exchange strategies of significant steel-delivering nations, and financial circumstances. The vacillation in steel costs can influence the benefit of Indian steel organizations and upset worldwide exchange elements.

Protectionist measures and exchange hindrances carried out by different nations represent another test. Hostile to unloading obligations and duties on steel imports have been forced by a few countries, including the US and the European Association. These actions can influence India's steel sends out and require an essential way to deal with explore exchange questions.

Natural worries are likewise a developing issue for the steel business. As the world pushes toward maintainable and eco-accommodating practices, steel organizations in India are feeling the squeeze to lessen their carbon impression and take on cleaner creation techniques. The reception of energy-effective advancements and carbon decrease measures is crucial for fulfill worldwide ecological guidelines and stay serious in the global steel market.

International elements can altogether affect India's steel exchange elements. Relations between nations can influence exchange, and political pressures can prompt changes in exchange arrangements and limitations. For instance, international strains among India and China have affected steel exchange elements between the two countries.

Wasteful operations and foundation can upset the seriousness of Indian steel organizations in the worldwide market. Opportune and practical transportation is basic for conveying steel items to worldwide clients. Further developing framework, including ports and transportation organizations, can improve the productivity of steel sends out.

Future Possibilities:

The fate of India's steel exchange elements is probably going to be formed by a mix of homegrown strategies, worldwide market patterns, and mechanical headways. To keep up with and reinforce its situation in the worldwide steel industry, India should address these difficulties and seek after the accompanying possibilities:

Expansion of Steel Items: India can extend its steel item portfolio to satisfy the developing needs of worldwide business sectors. Creating imaginative items and specialty sections can give open doors to development and separation.

Interest in Innovative work: Nonstop innovative work endeavors are important to work on the quality, effectiveness, and manageability of steel creation. Advancements in materials and cycles can improve India's seriousness.

Maintainable Works on: Sticking to manageable and harmless to the ecosystem practices will be pivotal. Decreasing fossil fuel byproducts, advancing asset usage, and embracing cleaner advancements can assist India with fulfilling worldwide natural guidelines.

Foundation Advancement: Interest in framework, including transportation, planned operations, and port offices, is fundamental to smooth out the commodity cycle and further develop proficiency.

Respective and Multilateral Arrangements: India can investigate two-sided economic deals and organizations with key exchanging accomplices to get a steady and developing business sector for its steel sends out. Furthermore, cooperation in worldwide discussions and associations can assist with tending to worldwide exchange difficulties.

Financial Enhancement: Advancing monetary broadening can decrease India's dependence on steel commodities and make the economy less powerless against variances in worldwide steel interest and costs.

Expertise Improvement: A talented labor force is fundamental to work and oversee progressed steel creation processes. Interest in expertise improvement and professional preparation can guarantee a certified labor force in the steel business.

7.2 The significance of global market integration.

Worldwide market mix, the cycle through which nations and economies become more interconnected with regards to exchange, money, and venture, has been a characterizing element of the cutting edge financial scene. This peculiarity has changed the manner in which countries direct business, shape their arrangements, and cooperate with each other. In this exposition, we will investigate the meaning of worldwide market mix, breaking down its authentic advancement, the advantages and difficulties it presents, and the ramifications for what's to come.

Authentic Development:

The underlying foundations of worldwide market reconciliation can be followed back to the earliest types of global exchange, where antiquated civilizations participated in the trading of products across tremendous distances. Nonetheless, the later and quick speed increase of worldwide market joining can be credited to a few critical verifiable turns of events:

Expansionism and Dominion: The European provincial powers of the sixteenth to nineteenth hundreds of years assumed a critical part in extending worldwide market joining. They laid out huge domains that worked with the development of products, work, and capital across mainlands. The double-dealing of settlements and the extraction of assets to serve the pilgrim powers established the groundwork for financial interdependencies on a worldwide scale.

Modern Upset: The Modern Transformation in the eighteenth and nineteenth hundreds of years got huge mechanical headways and upgrades transportation, empowering the large scale manufacturing and conveyance of products. It denoted a defining moment in worldwide exchange, as nations turned out to be progressively dependent on one another for natural substances and markets for completed items.

twentieth Century Foundations: The fallout of The Second Great War saw the foundation of establishments like the Global Money related Asset (IMF), the World Bank, and the Overall Settlement on Taxes and Exchange (GATT), which later advanced into the World Exchange Association (WTO). These associations expected to advance monetary participation and exchange progression, making way for expanded worldwide market incorporation.

Mechanical Progressions: The last 50% of the twentieth century got fast headways data innovation, broadcast communications, and transportation. The coming of the web and compartment transporting upset supply chains and diminished the expense of worldwide exchange, making worldwide market reconciliation more open and effective.

Advantages of Worldwide Market Coordination:

The meaning of worldwide market combination is highlighted by the bunch of advantages it offers to nations, organizations, and purchasers. A portion of the key benefits include:

Monetary Development: Incorporation into the worldwide market permits nations to get to bigger customer bases, animating financial development. Sending out items and administrations to worldwide business sectors can help a country's Gross domestic product and make occupations.

Proficiency and Specialization: Worldwide market mix empowers nations to spend significant time in the development of labor and products in which they enjoy a similar benefit. This specialization brings about more effective asset portion and higher efficiency.

Purchaser Decision: Shoppers benefit from worldwide market mix by accessing a more extensive assortment of items and administrations from various regions of the planet. This expanded rivalry frequently prompts lower costs and more excellent products.

Advancement and Innovation Move: Openness to global business sectors cultivates development and energizes innovation move. Firms should adjust and update their items and cycles to stay serious universally.

Speculation Open doors: Reconciliation draws in unfamiliar direct venture (FDI) as financial backers look for open doors in nations with open and available business sectors. FDI can invigorate monetary turn of events and occupation creation.

Risk Broadening: Expansion of business sectors and exchanging accomplices can assist nations with lessening monetary dangers related with reliance on a solitary market. This expansion balances out economies during worldwide financial slumps.

Difficulties of Worldwide Market Combination:

While worldwide market mix offers critical advantages, it likewise presents difficulties and dangers that nations and economies should oversee really. A portion of the noticeable difficulties include:

Pay Imbalance: Worldwide market incorporation can compound pay disparity inside nations. Laborers in ventures confronting expanded contest from worldwide business sectors might encounter work relocation and compensation stagnation.

Weakness to Outside Shocks: Economies vigorously dependent on worldwide exchange are powerless to outer shocks, for example, exchange debates, worldwide financial emergencies, and disturbances in worldwide stockpile chains, as shown by the Coronavirus pandemic.

Social and Social Effect: The flood of unfamiliar items and social impacts can raise worries about the conservation of nearby culture and customs. A view globalization as a danger to neighborhood characters.

Natural Effect: Expanded exchange can prompt ecological difficulties, like higher fossil fuel byproducts from transportation and impractical asset extraction. Finding some kind of harmony between financial development and ecological manageability is a significant test.

International Strains: International debates can upset worldwide exchange and make vulnerability for organizations. Exchange wars and protectionist measures can adversely affect worldwide market joining.

Administrative Harmonization: Contrasting administrative guidelines across nations can make obstructions to exchange. Blending guidelines and norms is an intricate interaction that requires participation between countries.

Suggestions for What's to come:

The meaning of worldwide market mix is ready to stay a focal subject before very long, as nations keep on exploring the intricacies of an interconnected world. The fate of worldwide market mix is probably going to be formed by a few key variables:

Mechanical Headways: Continuous innovative developments, like man-made consciousness, blockchain, and 5G, will additionally change the worldwide market scene. These advancements can possibly improve production network effectiveness, diminish expenses, and open new roads for exchange.

Environmental Change and Supportability: The basic of tending to environmental change and advancing manageability will impact worldwide market coordination. There will be a developing accentuation on naturally capable exchange rehearses, for example, carbon estimating and maintainable stockpile chains.

Advanced Exchange: The computerized economy is extending quickly, with advanced exchange administrations and advanced merchandise turning out to be progressively significant. Guidelines and arrangements overseeing computerized exchange, information protection, and network safety will assume a huge part.

International Realignment: International movements and realignments, especially with regards to the competition between significant powers, will keep on affecting worldwide market incorporation. Nations might reconsider their exchange approaches and collusions reaction to international turns of events.

Economic accords: Two-sided and multilateral economic accords will stay fundamental for nations looking to get market access and diminish exchange hindrances. Arrangements like the Thorough and Moderate Understanding for Transoceanic Association (CPTPP) and the Territorial Extensive Monetary Organization (RCEP) will shape exchange elements.

Comprehensive Exchange: There will be a developing accentuation on comprehensive exchange, with an emphasis on tending to pay disparity and social effects. Arrangements and arrangements might consolidate measures to guarantee that the advantages of worldwide market joining are dispersed all the more impartially.

7.3 Challenges and opportunities in a competitive global market.

The serious worldwide market is a consistently developing field where organizations, economies, and countries should explore a perplexing scene described by furious rivalry, innovative progressions, changing purchaser inclinations, and financial interdependencies. In this article, we will investigate the difficulties and open doors that emerge in this powerful climate, diving into the elements that shape the serious worldwide market and the systems that can assist substances with flourishing inside it.

Challenges in the Serious Worldwide Market

Serious Contest: One of the principal challenges in a cutthroat worldwide market is the sheer power of rivalry. Organizations from around the world compete for piece of the pie, and obstructions to passage are in many cases low, prompting swarmed and furiously challenged areas. More modest organizations might find it trying to rival laid out worldwide monsters, while bigger firms should ceaselessly develop to keep up with their strategic advantage.

Mechanical Disturbance: Fast innovative progressions, especially in the computerized area, have upset customary plans of action. Organizations that neglect to adjust to new advances can immediately become outdated. Keeping up to date with mechanical patterns and putting resources into advanced change is fundamental for endurance and development.

Worldwide Monetary Vulnerability: Monetary instability and vulnerability, exacerbated by occasions like the worldwide monetary emergency and the Coronavirus pandemic, present huge difficulties. Variances in cash trade rates, loan fees, and ware costs can upset field-tested strategies and dissolve benefits. Associations should foster strong methodologies to explore these vulnerabilities.

Store network Weaknesses: The worldwide inventory network has become progressively perplexing, depending on numerous providers across various nations. While this offers cost efficiencies, it additionally makes supply anchors powerless against interruptions, like catastrophic events, international strains, and pandemics. Organizations should improve inventory network versatility by enhancing providers and embracing progressed risk the executives rehearses.

Exchange Boundaries and Taxes: The reappearance of protectionist estimates as levies and exchange obstructions presents difficulties for worldwide organizations. Exchange questions between significant economies can disturb laid out supply chains and effect businesses going from agribusiness to innovation. Firms need to screen exchange approaches and consider emergency courses of action.

Administrative Intricacy: The administrative scene in the worldwide market is multi-layered and likely to change. Conforming to assorted guidelines, especially in areas like money, medical care, and the climate, can challenge. Lawful and consistence groups assume a pivotal part in assisting organizations with exploring this intricacy.

Social and Social Contrasts: Worldwide development frequently expects organizations to work in socially assorted conditions. Understanding and regarding social subtleties and accepted practices is crucial for building trust and effectively leading business. Organizations that overlook these distinctions risk harming their standing and confronting opposition from nearby partners.

Natural Maintainability: The basic of ecological manageability is filling in significance. Purchasers, financial backers, and state run administrations are progressively requesting eco-accommodating practices and items. Organizations should embrace practical techniques, diminish carbon impressions, and integrate green drives into their tasks to stay serious and meet administrative necessities.

Information Security and Online protection: In an interconnected world, information protection and network safety are fundamental worries. Breaks can prompt reputational harm, monetary misfortunes, and legitimate repercussions. Associations should put resources into strong network safety measures, shield shopper information, and remain consistent with information security regulations.

Open doors in the Serious Worldwide Market

Admittance to Worldwide Business sectors: Maybe the main open door in the serious worldwide market is the entrance it gives to a huge swath of customers. Entering global business sectors can permit organizations to take advantage of beforehand undiscovered income streams and grow their client base.

Mechanical Headways: While innovation can be a test, it likewise presents innumerable open doors. Progressions in computerization, man-made brainpower, and information examination can upgrade functional proficiency, drive advancement, and make new plans of action.

Advancement and Separation: The serious worldwide market rewards development and separation. Organizations that offer remarkable items or administrations for sale to the public, whether through mechanical development or imaginative plan, can cut out a specialty and flourish in a jam-packed scene.

Cooperative Associations: Cooperative associations with different organizations or associations can open up new open doors. These unions can give admittance to correlative assets, extend market reach, and cultivate development.

Monetary Development and Developing Business sectors: Developing business sectors offer open doors for organizations to gain by developing shopper interest. Organizations can lay out a presence in these business sectors and ride the rush of financial development, which might dominate mature business sectors.

Online business and Digitalization: The ascent of online business and digitalization presents open doors for organizations to arrive at a worldwide client base without the requirement for broad actual foundation. Online deals and computerized showcasing empower more modest endeavors to contend on a worldwide scale.

Manageability as an Upper hand: Embracing maintainability practices can be a huge upper hand. Organizations that embrace harmless to the ecosystem procedures and straightforwardly impart their obligation to supportability can draw in ecologically cognizant buyers and financial backers.

Worldwide Ability Pool: The worldwide market gives admittance to a different and exceptionally gifted ability pool. Organizations can use this ability to drive development, help efficiency, and accomplish an upper hand.

Techniques for Outcome in the Cutthroat Worldwide Market

Nonstop Development: Organizations should focus on advancement to remain in front of the opposition. Putting resources into innovative work, encouraging a culture of imagination, and embracing arising advances are key parts of development methodologies.

Statistical surveying: Extensive statistical surveying is fundamental to figure out purchaser inclinations, administrative conditions, and social subtleties in target markets. This information empowers organizations to fit their items and administrations to neighborhood needs.

Inventory network Enhancement: Building a tough production network is essential. Enhancing providers, putting resources into stock administration, and executing risk relief techniques can assist with limiting interruptions and keep a consistent progression of merchandise.

Administrative Consistence: Organizations should lay areas of strength for out and consistence groups to explore complex administrative conditions. They ought to remain informed about changes parents in law and guidelines and adjust their tasks as needs be.

Network safety Measures: Hearty online protection measures, including encryption, normal reviews, and representative preparation, are basic to shield delicate information. Laying out an episode reaction plan is fundamental to answer really to information breaks.

Manageability Drives: Embracing maintainability practices can work on an organization's natural impression as well as upgrade its standing. Numerous buyers and financial backers effectively support organizations that show a guarantee to manageability.

Worldwide Extension Techniques: Cautiously think about the strategy for worldwide development. Choices incorporate product, joint endeavors, consolidations and acquisitions, and diversifying. The decision relies upon the idea of the business, target markets, and accessible assets.

Social Ability: Creating social capability among representatives and initiative is urgent. Diverse preparation can help people comprehend and regard social contrasts, encouraging better correspondence and associations with neighborhood partners.

Client Driven Approach: In a cutthroat worldwide market, it is fundamental to zero in on consumer loyalty. A client driven approach, joined with criticism instruments, assists organizations with adjusting to changing purchaser inclinations.

Dexterous and Versatile Mentality: A spry and versatile outlook is fundamental to flourish in a quickly evolving climate. Organizations ought to support adaptability, fast navigation, and the capacity to turn because of market shifts.